Forest Health Monitoring 2006 National Technical Report

Editors Mark J. Ambrose Barbara L. Conkling

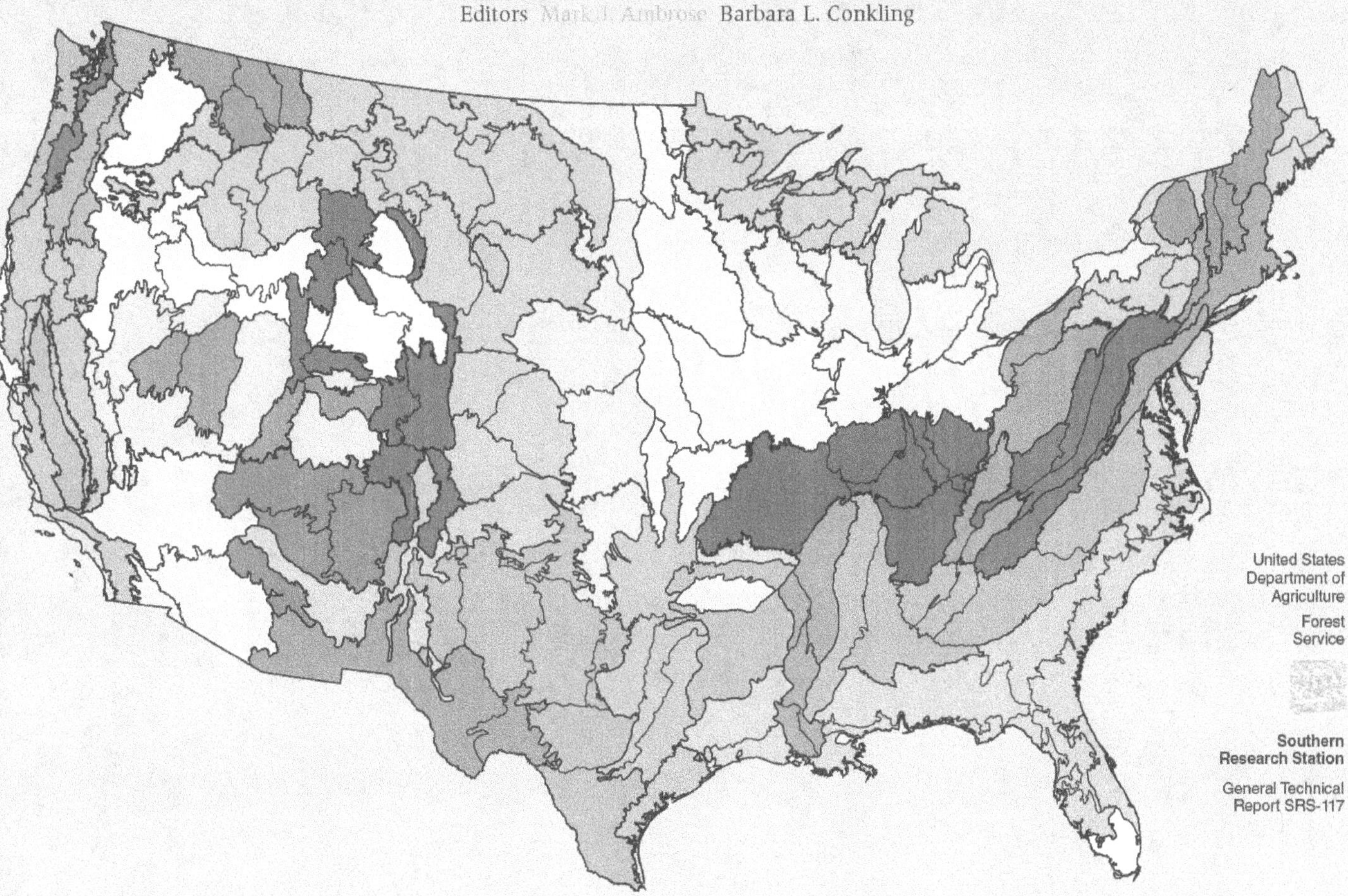

United States
Department of
Agriculture

Forest
Service

Southern
Research Station

General Technical
Report SRS-117

Front cover map: Ecoregion provinces
and ecoregion sections for the continental
United States (Cleland and others 2005).

Back cover map: Forest land (green)
backdrop derived from Advanced Very High
Resolution Radiometer satellite imagery
(Zhu and Evans 1994).

July 2009
Southern Research Station
200 W.T. Weaver Blvd.
Asheville, NC 28804

Forest Health Monitoring 2006 National Technical Report

Editors

Mark J. Ambrose, Research Assistant, North Carolina State University, Department of Forestry and Environmental Resources, Raleigh, NC 27695

Barbara L. Conkling, Research Assistant Professor, North Carolina State University, Department of Forestry and Environmental Resources, Raleigh, NC 27695

Abstract

The Forest Health Monitoring Program's annual national technical report presents results of forest health analyses from a national perspective using data from a variety of sources. The report is organized according to the Criteria and Indicators for the Conservation and Sustainable Management of Temperate and Boreal Forests of the Santiago Declaration. Drought in 2005 is presented, and drought over the decade 1996–2005 is compared with the historical average. The relationship between lightning frequency and forest fire occurrence is investigated. National air pollution data are used to estimate the exposure of forests to ozone, wet sulfate deposition, and wet deposition of inorganic nitrogen. Baseline results of lichens, as an indicator of air pollution in the Pacific Northwest, are presented. Aerial survey data are used to identify hotspots of insect and disease activity based on the relative exposure to defoliation- and mortality-causing agents. Marine cargo data are analyzed to identify locations where exotic insect pests are likely to be introduced. Forest Inventory and Analysis crown condition data are analyzed to identify spatial clusters of plots where trees have relatively poor crowns, which might indicate forest health problems.

Keywords—Air pollution, criteria and indicators, crowns, drought, fire, lichens.

ii

Table of Contents

Contents, cont.

List of Figures

List of Tables

This annual technical report is a product of the Forest Health Monitoring (FHM) Program. The report provides information about a variety of issues relating to forest health at a national scale. FHM national reports have the dual focus of presenting analyses of the latest available data and showcasing innovative techniques for analyzing forest health data. The report is organized using the Criteria and Indicators for the Conservation and Sustainable Management of Temperate and Boreal Forests (Anon. 1995) as a general reporting framework.

While FHM is committed to reporting annually on the state of U.S. forests, there are not always enough new data available to warrant reporting on each indicator every year. In this report, indicators are included if a substantial amount of new data has become available since they were last reported by FHM, or if progress in the development and application of analytical techniques has enabled FHM to use the data to provide new insights into the health of U.S. forests. Earlier reports have strongly focused on indicators of forest condition and on levels of stressors that may be affecting forest health. In this report we also examine some of the mechanisms behind the stressors that affect U.S. forests, including the relationship of lightning to forest fires and pathways by which exotic insect pests can be introduced.

The Forest Health Monitoring Program

The FHM Program is a national effort to determine on an annual basis the status of, and changes and trends in, indicators of forest condition. The Forest Service, U.S. Department of Agriculture cooperates with State forestry and agricultural agencies to conduct FHM activities. Other Federal Agencies and universities also participate. The FHM Program has five major activities (Tkacz 2003):

- Detection monitoring—nationally standardized aerial and ground surveys to evaluate status and change in condition of forest ecosystems
- Evaluation monitoring—projects to determine extent, severity, and causes of undesirable changes in forest health identified through detection monitoring
- Intensive site monitoring—to enhance understanding of cause and effect relationships by linking detection monitoring to ecosystem process studies and to assess specific issues, such as calcium depletion and carbon sequestration, at multiple spatial scales

Chapter 1. Introduction

MARK J. AMBROSE

- Research on monitoring techniques—to develop or improve indicators, monitoring systems, and analytical techniques, such as urban and riparian forest health monitoring, early detection of invasive species, multivariate analyses of forest health indicators, and spatial scan statistics
- Analysis and reporting—synthesis of information from various data sources within and external to the Forest Service to produce issue-driven reports on the status of and change in forest health at national, regional, and State levels

In addition to FHM's national reporting, each of the five FHM regions, as well as FHM's partners both within the Forest Service and in State forestry departments, also produce reports. The regions, in cooperation with their respective States, produce "Forest Health Highlights" (available on the FHM Web site at www.fhm. fs.fed.us); State reports such as Keyes and others (2003), Laustsen and others (2003), Neitlich and others (2003), Steinman (2004), and Snyder (2006); and other forest health reports, such as Morin and others (2006) and Cumming and others (2006). FHM and its partners also produce reports on monitoring techniques and analytical methods, such as Smith and Conkling (2004) and O'Neill and others (2005).

Data Sources

The FHM Program strives to use a variety of data collected by the various branches of the Forest Service as well as data from other sources. A major data source is the Forest Service's Forest Inventory and Analysis (FIA) Program. The FIA Program's phase 2 consists of plots measured at regular intervals to collect data associated with traditional forest inventories. FIA's phase 3 plots are a subset of the phase 2 plots. On phase 3 plots additional data are collected on many of the forest health indicators that were previously measured as part of the FHM detection monitoring ground plot system (Palmer and others 1991).[1]

For this report, Forest Service data sources were: FIA periodic inventory and annualized phase 2 survey data (1990–2003)[2]; FIA phase 3 data—crown condition (2000–04), lichens (1998–2003); and Forest Health Protection (FHP) aerial survey data

---

[1] U.S. Department of Agriculture Forest Service. 1998. Forest health monitoring 1998 field methods guide. Research Triangle Park, NC: U.S. Department of Agriculture Forest Service, National Forest Health Monitoring Program, 473 p. On file with: Forest Health Monitoring Program National Office, 3041 Cornwallis Road, Research Triangle Park, NC 27709.

[2] U.S. Department of Agriculture Forest Service, Forest Inventory and Analysis National Office,1601 North Kent Street, Suite 400, Arlington, VA 22209. http://fia.fs.fed.us/tools-data/data/. [Date accessed: September 1, 2005].

(1998–2004).[3] Other data sources were: National Aeronautics and Space Administration (NASA)—lightning data (Global Hydrology Resource Center 2004); National Oceanic and Atmospheric Administration—Palmer Drought Severity Index (1895 through 2005) (National Climatic Data Center 1994); moderate resolution imaging spectroradiometer (MODIS) fire data for 2001–05 (Forest Service, Remote Sensing Application Center 2006); National Interagency Coordination Center (2004) data on forest area burned in 2005, U.S. Army Corps of Engineers Navigation Data Center (2005)—marine cargo data (1997–2003); and U.S. Department of Transportation, Bureau of Transportation Statistics and U.S. Department of Commerce, U.S. Census Bureau (2005)—commodity flow data.

About the Report

In this report we used the Santiago Declaration and accompanying criteria and indicators (Anon. 1995, Montreal Process Working Group 1999) that were adopted by the Forest Service as a forest sustainability assessment framework (Smith and others 2001, U.S. Department of Agriculture Forest Service 2004). The seven criteria are:

Criterion 1—conservation of biological diversity

Criterion 2—maintenance of productive capacity of forest ecosystems

Criterion 3—maintenance of forest ecosystem health and vitality

Criterion 4—conservation and maintenance of soil and water resources

Criterion 5—maintenance of forest contribution to global carbon cycles

Criterion 6—maintenance and enhancement of long-term multiple socioeconomic benefits to meet the needs of societies

Criterion 7—legal, institutional, and economic framework for forest conservation and sustainable management

A complete evaluation of all the sustainability criteria is not appropriate here. We focus on criterion 3, which is directly related to issues of forest health.

Bailey's ecoregion sections and provinces (Bailey 1995) as revised (Cleland and others 2005) were used as the assessment units for analysis (fig. 1.1)[4] when the spatial scale of the

---

[3] U.S. Department of Agriculture Forest Service, Forest Health Technology Enterprise Team. Unpublished database. On file with: FHP/FHTET, 2150 Centre Avenue, Building A, Suite 331, Fort Collins, CO 80526–1891.

[4] Chapter 5, "Baseline Results from the Lichen Community Indicator Program in the Pacific Northwest: Air Quality Patterns and Evidence of a Nitrogen Pollution Problem," is an exception. The analyst used an earlier version of Bailey's ecoregion section delineations (McNab and Avers 1994) to be consistent with the results of earlier lichen analyses referenced.

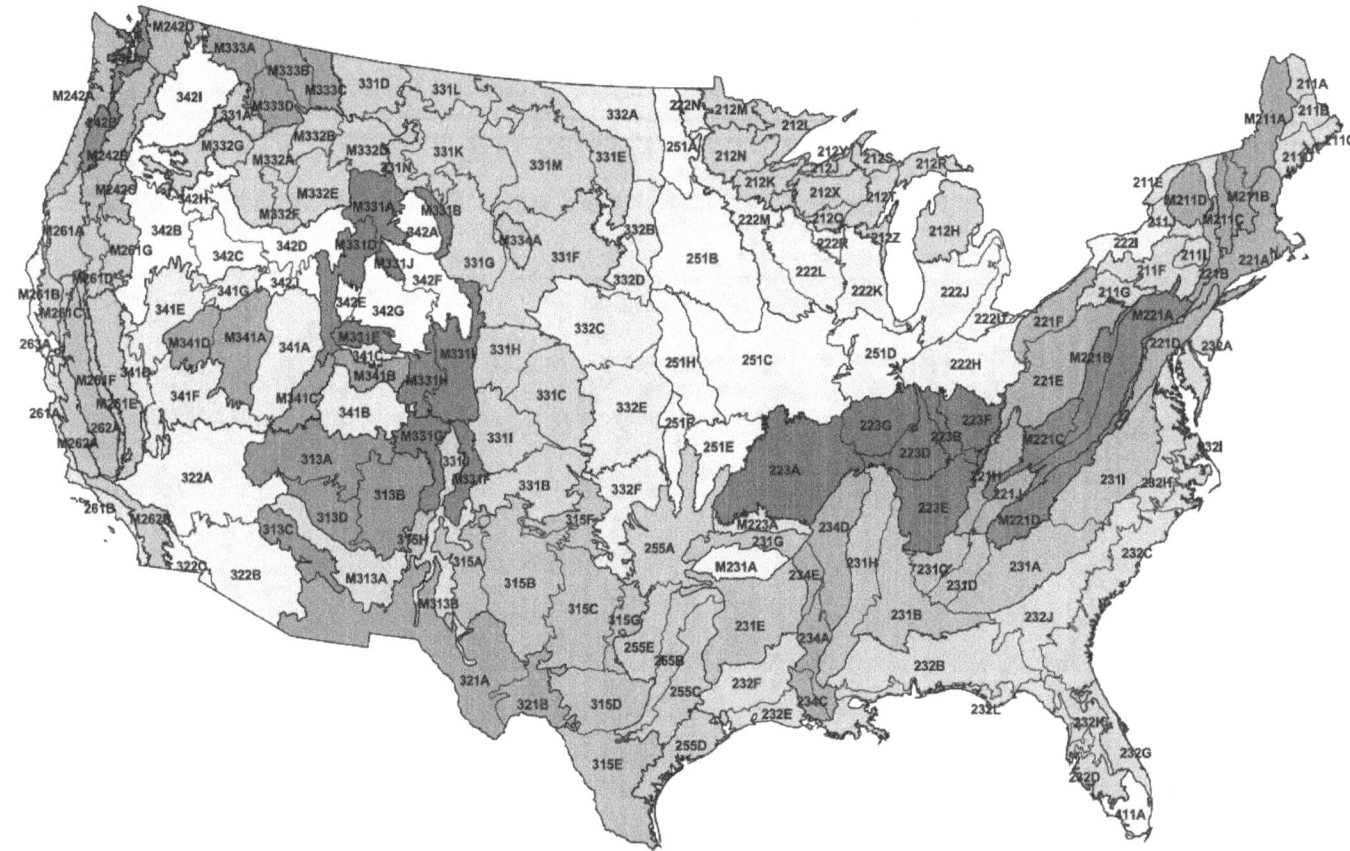

Figure 1.1—Ecoregion provinces and ecoregion sections for the continental United States (Cleland and others 2005). Ecoregion sections within each ecoregion province are shown in the same color.

Eastern ecoregion provinces

Adirondack—New England Mixed Forest—Coniferous Forest—Alpine Meadow (M211)
Central Appalachian Broadleaf Forest—Coniferous Forest—Meadow (M221)
Central Interior Broadleaf Forest (223)
Eastern Broadleaf Forest (221)
Everglades (411)
Laurentian Mixed Forest (212)
Lower Mississippi Riverine Forest (234)
Midwest Broadleaf Forest (222)
Northeastern Mixed Forest (211)
Ouachita Mixed Forest—Meadow (M231)
Outer Coastal Plain Mixed Forest (232)
Ozark Broadleaf Forest (M223)
Prairie Parkland (Subtropical) (255)
Prairie Parkland (Temperate) (251)
Southeastern Mixed Forest (231)

Western ecoregion provinces

American Semi-Desert and Desert (322)
Arizona—New Mexico Mountains Semi-Desert—Open Woodland—Coniferous Forest—Alpine Meadow (M313)
Black Hills Coniferous Forest (M334)
California Coastal Chapparal Forest and Shrub (261)
California Coastal Range Open Woodland—Shrub—Coniferous Forest—Meadow (M262)
California Coastal Steppe, Mixed Forest, and Redwood Forest (263)
California Dry Steppe (262)
Cascade Mixed Forest—Coniferous Forest—Alpine Meadow (M242)
Chihuahuan Semi-Desert (321)
Colorado Plateau Semi-Desert (313)
Great Plains—Palouse Dry Steppe (331)
Great Plains Steppe (332)
Intermountain Semi-Desert (342)
Intermountain Semi-Desert and Desert (341)
Middle Rocky Mountains Steppe—Coniferous Forest—Alpine Meadow (M332)
Nevada—Utah Mountains—Semi-Desert—Coniferous Forest—Alpine Meadow (M341)
Northern Rocky Mountains Forest—Steppe—Coniferous Forest—Alpine Meadow (M333)
Pacific Lowland Mixed Forest (242)
Sierran Steppe—Mixed Forest—Coniferous Forest—Alpine Meadow (M261)
Southern Rocky Mountains Steppe—Open Woodland—Coniferous Forest—Alpine Meadow (M331)
Southwest Plateau and Plains Dry Steppe and Shrub (315)

available data made such analyses appropriate and when the indicator being analyzed could reasonably be expected to show some pattern relating to ecological regions. This is a national, hierarchical system of ecological units that classifies the United States into ecoregion domains, divisions, provinces, sections, subsections, landtype associations, and landtypes (McNab and others 2005). Ecoregion sections typically contain thousands of square miles. Areas within an ecoregion section are expected to be similar in their geology and lithology, regional climate, soils, potential natural vegetation, and potential natural communities (Cleland and others 1997). Ecoregion sections provide a common framework for an ecologically based assessment.

Literature Cited

Anon. 1995. Sustaining the world's forests: the Santiago agreement. Journal of Forestry. 93: 18–21.

Bailey, R.G. 1995. Descriptions of the ecoregions of the United States. 2d ed. Misc. Publ.1391. Washington, DC: U.S. Department of Agriculture Forest Service. 108 p. [Map scale 1:7,500,000].

Cleland, D.T.; Avers, P.E.; McNab, W.H. [and others]. 1997. National hierarchical framework of ecological units. In: Boyce, M.S.; Haney, A.. eds. Ecosystem management applications for sustainable forest and wildlife resources. New Haven, CT: Yale University Press: 181–200.

Cleland, D.T.; Freeouf, J.A.; Keys, J.E. [and others]. 2005. Ecological subregions: sections and subsections for the conterminous United States. Washington, DC: U.S. Department of Agriculture Forest Service. Map, presentation scale 1:3,500,000; colored]. [Also on CD–ROM as a Geographic Information System coverage in ArcINFO format].

Cumming, A.B.; Twardus, D.B.; Smith, W.D. 2006. National forest health monitoring program, Maryland and Massachusetts street tree monitoring pilot projects. NA–FR–01–06. Newtown Square, PA: U.S. Department of Agriculture Forest Service, Northeastern Area, State and Private Forestry. 23 p.

Keyes, C.; Rogers, P.; LaMadeleine, L. [and others]. 2003. Utah forest health report: a baseline assessment, 1999–2001. Salt Lake City: Utah Department of Natural Resources, Division of Forestry, Fire and State Lands. 47 p.

Laustsen, K.M.; Griffith, D.M.; Steinman, J.R. 2003. Fourth annual inventory report on Maine's forests. Augusta, ME: Maine Forest Service; Newtown Square, PA: U.S. Department of Agriculture Forest Service, Northeastern Research Station and Northeastern Area. 49 p. http://mainegov-images.informe.org/doc/mfs/pubs/pdf/anninv/2002invrpt.pdf. [Date accessed: June 22, 2004].

McNab, W.H.; Avers, P.E., comps. 1994. Ecological subregions of the United States: section descriptions. WO–WSA–5. Washington, DC: U.S. Department of Agriculture Forest Service. 267 p.

McNab, W.H.; Cleland, D.T.; Freeouf, J.A. [and others], comps. 2005. Description of ecological subregions: sections of the conterminous United States [CD–ROM]. Washington, DC: U.S. Department of Agriculture Forest Service. 80 p.

Montreal Process Working Group. 1999. Criteria and indicators for the conservation and sustainable management of temperate and boreal forests: Montreal process. 2^d ed. Montreal, Canada: Montreal Process Working Group; Ottawa, Canada: Canadian Forest Service. 19 p. http://www.mpci.org/rep-pub/1999/1999santiago_e.pdf and http://www.mpci.org/rep-pub/1999/ci_e.html. [Date accessed: July 18, 2006].

Morin, R.S.; Liebhold, A.M.; Gottschalk, K.W. [and others]. 2006. Analysis of forest health monitoring surveys on the Allegheny National Forest (1998–2001). Gen. Tech. Rep. NE–339. Newtown Square, PA: U.S. Department of Agriculture Forest Service, Northeastern Research Station. 102 p. http://www.fs.fed.us/ne/newtown_square/publications/technical_reports/pdfs/2006/ne_gtr339.pdf. [Date accessed: September 13].

National Aeronautics and Space Administration, Global Hydrology Resource Center. 2004. LIS/OTD 0.5-degree high resolution full climatology. http://ghrc.msfc.nasa.gov/. [Date accessed: March 7, 2006].

National Climatic Data Center. 1994. Time bias corrected divisional temperature-precipitation-drought index. Documentation for dataset TD–9640. On file with: Database Management Branch, National Climatic Data Center, National Oceanic and Atmospheric Administration, Federal Building, 37 Battery Park Avenue, Asheville, NC 28801–2733. 12 p. http://www.ncdc.noaa.gov/oa/climate/onlineprod/drought/readme.html. [Date accessed: unknown].

National Interagency Coordination Center. 2004. National Interagency Coordination Center 2004 statistics and summary. Boise, ID: National Interagency Fire Center. 10 p. http://www.nifc.gov/news/2004_statssumm/intro_summary.pdf. [Date accessed: May 13, 2005].

Neitlich, P.; Rogers, P.; Rosentretter, R. 2003. Lichen communities indicator results from Idaho: baseline sampling. Gen. Tech. Rep. RMRS–GTR–103. Fort Collins, CO: U.S. Department of Agriculture Forest Service, Rocky Mountain Research Station. 14 p.

O'Neill, K.P.; Amacher, M.C.; Perry, C.H. 2005. Soils as an indicator of forest health: a guide to the collection, analysis, and interpretation of soil indicator data in the forest inventory and analysis program. Gen. Tech. Rep. NC–258. St. Paul, MN: U.S. Department of Agriculture Forest Service, North Central Research Station. 53 p.

Palmer, C.J.; Riitters, K.H.; Strickland, T. [and others]. 1991. Monitoring and research strategy for forests - environmental monitoring and assessment program (EMAP). EPA/600/4–91/012. Washington, DC: U.S. Environmental Protection Agency. 187 p.

Smith, W.B.; Vissage, J.S.; Darr, D.R.; Sheffield, R.M. 2001. Forest resources of the United States, 1997. Gen. Tech. Rep. NC–219. St. Paul, MN: U.S. Department of Agriculture Forest Service, North Central Research Station. 191 p.

Smith, W.D.; Conkling, B.L. 2004. Analyzing forest health data. Gen. Tech. Rep. SRS–077. Asheville, NC: U.S. Department of Agriculture Forest Service, Southern Research Station. 33 p. http://www.srs.fs.usda.gov/pubs/gtr/gtr_srs077.pdf. [Date accessed: July 17, 2006].

Snyder, C., comp. 2006. Forest health conditions in Alaska – 2005. Prot. Rep. R10–PR–5. Anchorage, AK: U.S. Department of Agriculture Forest Service, Alaska Region; State of Alaska, Department of Natural Resources, Forestry Division. 92 p.

Steinman, J. 2004. Forest health monitoring in the Northeastern United States: disturbances and conditions during 1993–2002. NA–Tech. Pap. 01–04. Newtown Square, PA: U.S. Department of Agriculture Forest Service, State and Private Forestry, Northeastern Area. 46 p. http://fhm.fs.fed.us/pubs/tp/dist_cond/dc.shtm. [Date accessed: June 30, 2006].

Tkacz, B.M. 2003. Forest health monitoring program [factsheet]. Washington, DC: U.S. Department of Agriculture Forest Service, State and Private Forestry, Forest Health Protection. 2 p. http://www.fhm.fs.fed.us/fact/03/prog_desc.pdf. [Date accessed: May 18, 2005].

U.S. Army Corps of Engineers, Navigation Data Center. 2005. U.S. waterway data: foreign cargo (inbound and outbound) for 1997–2003. New Orleans, LA: U.S. Army Corps of Engineers, Navigation Data Center, Waterborne Commerce Statistics Center. http://www.iwr.usace.army.mil/ndc/data/dataimex.htm [Date accessed: October 23, 2006]

U.S. Department of Agriculture Forest Service. 2004. National report on sustainable forests—2003. FS–766. Washington, DC. 139 p.

U.S. Department of Agriculture, Forest Service, Remote Sensing Application Center. 2006. MODIS Active Fire Mapping Program: GIS data. Salt Lake City, UT: U.S. Department of Agriculture, Forest Service, Remote Sensing Application Center. http://activefiremaps.fs.fed.us/fireptdata.php [Date accessed: March 21]

U.S. Department of Transportation, Bureau of Transportation Statistics; U.S. Department of Commerce, U.S. Census Bureau. 2005. Commodity flow survey 2002 [CD–ROM]. C1–E02–ECFS–00–US1. Washington, DC.

Drought occurrence is a function of temperature, moisture, and soil characteristics. In some regions, such as much of the Western United States, drought is a regular occurrence, while in others, such as the Northeastern United States, drought occurs on an irregular basis. Moderate drought stress tends to slow plant growth while severe drought stress also reduces photosynthesis (Kareiva and others 1993).

Drought also interacts with other forest stressors. For example, Mattson and Haack (1987) identified 10 insect families that historically reach outbreak status following drought episodes. Drought also affects the level of damage plants receive due to ozone. Plant injury from elevated ozone exposure occurs during gas exchange, which is partially regulated by moisture. Under drought conditions plants close their stomates to conserve water. When stomates are closed, gas exchange does not occur, and plant injury from ozone does not result. Drought can also influence fire characteristics. For example, Taylor and Beaty (2005) found that drought intensity over a 200-year period (1650–1850) affected fire extent in the northern Sierra Nevada Mountains.

Brief Methods

The National Climatic Data Center (NCDC) calculates the Palmer Drought Severity Index (PDSI) monthly by climate division for the conterminous United States. The NCDC archive contains monthly estimates of PDSI from 1895 to present (National Climatic Data Center 1994). PDSI was used to examine drought occurrence at the single year (2005) and 10-year (1996–2005) time scales by ecoregion section (Cleland and others 2005). We considered "drought" to include PDSI values < –2.0, which indicates moderate, severe, and extreme drought conditions. The value for each ecoregion section was estimated using a forest area weighted average [see Conkling and others (2005) for more information]. Drought deviation was used to quantify drought over the last 10 years (Conkling and others 2005). Drought frequency from 1895 through 2005 served as a historical account or reference point for each ecoregion section. For example, if 333 months of drought were recorded in an ecoregion section from 1895 through 2005, then 30 months of drought would be expected on a 120-month (10-year) basis. The historical account was then compared to the

Chapter 2. Drought

John W. Coulston

current decade. If the expected number of months with drought conditions was 30, and 39 months of drought were recorded in the current decade, then the drought deviation was 39–30 = 9.

Results

In 2005, 51.1 percent of the ecoregion sections in the conterminous United States did not experience any moderate, severe, or extreme drought (fig. 2.1). Section 212R—Eastern Upper Peninsula in Michigan was the only section in the East that had more than 4 months of drought during 2005. In the Western United States, forests in both section M332D—Belt Mountains and section M334A—Black Hills experienced 8 months of drought. Also of note in the Western United States was section M332G—Blue Mountains in Oregon, which had 9 months of drought in 2005.

While 51.1 percent of ecoregion sections did not experience drought in 2005, several ecoregion sections had drier than expected conditions from 1996–2005 (fig. 2.2). Approximately 12 percent of the ecoregion sections experienced more than 24 additional months of drought than expected. Many of these sections were in the Western United States, and included sections M332D—Belt Mountains, M332A—Idaho Batholith, M332G—Blue Mountains, M331A—Yellowstone Highlands, and 313C—Tonto Transitions. Also of note was section 232K—Florida Coastal Plains Central Highlands, which had 19 more months of drought from 1996 to 2005 than expected. While several ecoregion sections experienced more drought than was expected, approximately 35 percent of the ecoregion sections experienced approximately the expected amount of drought (drought deviation = –5 to 6 months).

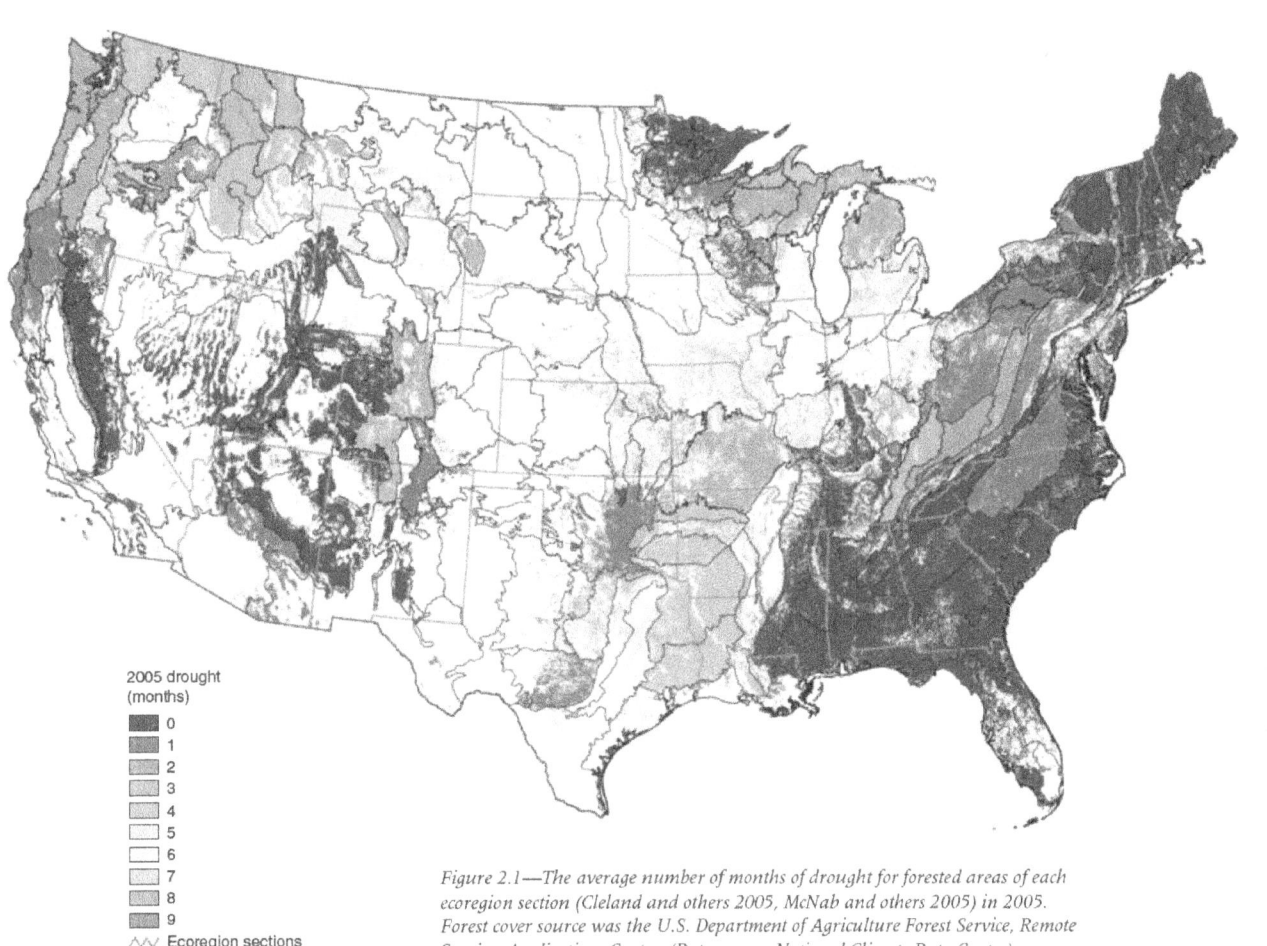

2005 drought
(months)

- 0
- 1
- 2
- 3
- 4
- 5
- 6
- 7
- 8
- 9

/\/\ Ecoregion sections
— States

Figure 2.1—The average number of months of drought for forested areas of each ecoregion section (Cleland and others 2005, McNab and others 2005) in 2005. Forest cover source was the U.S. Department of Agriculture Forest Service, Remote Sensing Applications Center. (Data source: National Climate Data Center)

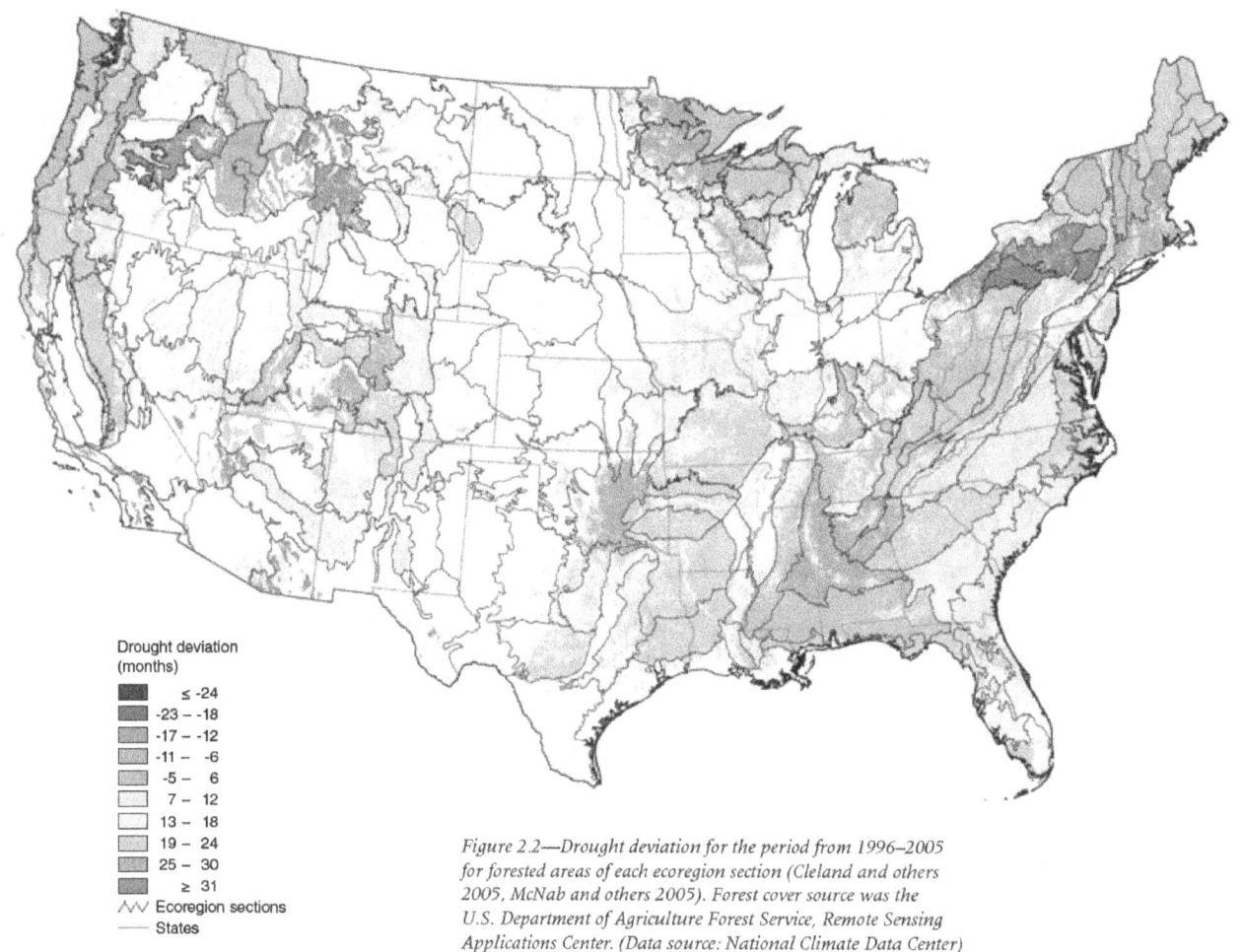

Drought deviation
(months)

≤ -24
-23 – -18
-17 – -12
-11 – -6
-5 – 6
7 – 12
13 – 18
19 – 24
25 – 30
≥ 31

∧∧∧ Ecoregion sections
⎯⎯ States

*Figure 2.2—Drought deviation for the period from 1996–2005
for forested areas of each ecoregion section (Cleland and others
2005, McNab and others 2005). Forest cover source was the
U.S. Department of Agriculture Forest Service, Remote Sensing
Applications Center. (Data source: National Climate Data Center)*

Literature Cited

Cleland, D.T.; Freeouf, J.A.; Keys, J.E. [and others]. 2005. Ecological subregions: sections and subsections for the conterminous United States. Washington, DC: U.S. Department of Agriculture Forest Service. [Map, presentation scale 1:3,500,000; colored]. [Also on CD-ROM as a Geographic Information System coverage in ArcINFO format].

Conkling, B.L.; Coulston, J.W.; Ambrose, M.J., eds. 2005. Forest health monitoring 2001 national technical report. Gen. Tech. Rep. SRS–81. Asheville, NC: U.S. Department of Agriculture Forest Service, Southern Research Station. 204 p.

Kareiva, P.M.; Kingsolver, J.G.; Huey, R.B., eds. 1993. Biotic interactions and global change. Sunderland, MA: Sinauer Associates Inc. 559 p.

Mattson, W.J.; Haack, R.A. 1987. The role of drought in outbreaks of plant-eating insects. BioScience. 37(2): 110–118.

McNab, W.H.; Cleland, D.T.; Freeouf, J.A. [and others], comps. 2005. Description of ecological subregions: sections of the conterminous United States [CD–ROM]. Washington, DC: U.S. Department of Agriculture Forest Service. 80 p.

National Climatic Data Center. 1994. Time bias corrected divisional temperature-precipitation-drought index. Documentation for dataset TD–9640. On file with: Database Management Branch, National Climatic Data Center, National Oceanic and Atmospheric Administration, Federal Building, 37 Battery Park Avenue, Asheville, NC 28801–2733. 12 p. http://www.ncdc.noaa.gov/oa/climate/onlineprod/drought/readme.html. [Date accessed: May 30, 2006].

Taylor, A.H.; Beaty, R.M. 2005. Climatic influences on fire regimes in the northern Sierra Nevada Mountains, Lake Tahoe Basin, Nevada, USA. Journal of Biogeography. 32(3): 425–438.

Why Is Lightning Important?

Lightning disturbance can affect forest health at various scales. Lightning strikes may kill or weaken individual trees. Lightning-damaged trees may in turn function as epicenters of pest outbreaks in forest stands, as is the case with the southern pine beetle and other bark beetles (Rykiel and others 1988). At a landscape scale, lightning greatly influences forest structure and composition by igniting wildfires. Lightning is the leading natural cause of wildfire ignitions worldwide (Vasquez and Moreno 1998) and is the leading overall cause of ignitions in the Western United States (Rorig and Ferguson 1999). Whether lightning-ignited wildfires expand to affect large areas depends on a number of environmental factors, including quantity and moisture content of fire fuels, climate and weather conditions, and fire suppression efforts (Rorig and Ferguson 2002). The relationship among climate, lightning, and fire is not well understood, and this relationship is further complicated by the preponderance of human-caused fires in some regions of the world (Morgan and others 2001, Vasquez and Moreno 1998).

National-scale fire and lightning-density spatial datasets, developed from remotely sensed sources, have recently become available for the United States. By examining the correlation between these datasets, it may be possible to identify regions of the United States where lightning density serves as a predictor of forest fire activity.

Methods

Moderate resolution imaging spectroradiometer (MODIS), mounted on 2 National Aeronautics and Space Administration (NASA) satellites (Aqua and Terra), has 36 spectral bands ranging from 0.4 to 14 μm (thermal infrared) in wavelength. Together, Aqua MODIS and Terra MODIS cover the mid-to-higher latitudes of the globe four times daily (National Aeronautics and Space Administration 2006). The Forest Service, NASA, and the University of Maryland have collaborated to produce daily active fire occurrence data using MODIS thermal infrared bands [see Giglio and others (2003) for a description of the data processing algorithm]. Data on fire occurrences since 2001 are available online from the Forest Service, Remote Sensing Applications Center (RSAC) (2006). The data are delivered as annual point coverages, where each

Chapter 3. Relating Lightning Data to Fire Occurrence Data

Frank H. Koch

point represents the center of a 1-km^2 cell where a fire was detected in a given year. The MODIS data do not depict the areal extent of fires, and so are best suited to regional- or national-scale assessments of fire pattern.

The NASA Global Hydrology Resource Center created a global map of mean annual lightning activity using data from two satellite-based sensors, the lightning imaging sensor (LIS) and the optical transient detector (OTD). Five years of LIS (1997–2002) and OTD (1995–2000) data were combined to create a raster map of total lightning activity, reported in terms of flash rate density (number of flashes km^{-2} per year) for 0.5-degree grid cells (NASA Global Hydrology Resource Center 2004). Total lightning activity can be divided into two subcategories: intracloud and cloud-to-ground discharges, with only the latter being relevant for fire ignitions. Estimating what proportion of the total lightning activity depicted by the LIS/OTD map consists of cloud-to-ground activity is difficult, as there is some broadscale geographic variation in the intracloud/cloud-to-ground ratio (Boccippio and others 2001). Nonetheless, the overall spatial

pattern of the LIS/OTD map is quite similar to maps generated using only cloud-to-ground lightning data from the U.S. National Lightning Detection Network (Zajac and Rutledge 2001), suggesting that it is appropriate for evaluating national-scale trends.

To facilitate comparison of these datasets, the LIS/OTD map was first clipped to the conterminous United States and reprojected from a geographic to an Albers conic equal-area projection. The map's original 0.5-degree cells were resampled to 50 km by 50 km (2500 km2) cells using a nearest neighbor approach. These cells served as the primary sampling units for measuring forest fire occurrence. For each cell, the total number of forest fires (2001–05) was determined by intersecting the MODIS active fire occurrence coverages for each year with a 1-km resolution forest cover map developed by RSAC from MODIS imagery. Only fires that occurred in forested areas depicted by the MODIS forest cover map were counted towards the 5-year total for each 2500-km2 cell. In addition, there were a number of partial cells along U.S. coastlines as well as the United States-Canada and United States-Mexico borders. For each partial cell i, the number of forest fire occurrences was area-adjusted using the formula

$$F'_i = \frac{F_i * 2500}{A_i}$$

where

F'_i = adjusted number of forest fire occurrences for cell i

F_i = original number of forest fire occurrences for cell i

A_i = actual land area of cell i in km^2

Each cell was labeled according to the ecoregion province in which its center point fell.

Spearman's rank-order correlations (Steel and others 1997) were calculated between lightning flash density and the number of forest fires per cell. This nonparametric correlation approach first ranks the data and then applies the standard, i.e., Pearson's, correlation equation to those ranks (SAS Institute 1999). Spearman's correlation coefficients were calculated for cells grouped by ecoregion province (Cleland and others 2005), for all cells in ecoregion provinces of the Eastern United States ($N = 1475$), and for all cells in ecoregion provinces of the Western United States ($N = 1598$) (fig. 3.1). Only cells that included some forested area based on the MODIS forest cover map were included in the correlation analyses. To provide perspective on the relative importance of lightning as a predictor, Spearman's rank-order correlations were similarly calculated between human

Figure 3.1—Eastern and Western United States super-regional groups for correlation testing. Gray lines are ecoregion provinces (Cleland and others 2005).

population density (number of individuals km^{-2}) and the number of forest fires per cell. Population density was calculated from U.S. Census 2000 population data mapped at the census block level (Environmental Systems Research Institute 2006).

What Do the Data Show?

The total number of forest fires in each 2500-km^2 cell between 2001 and 2005 (fig. 3.2) ranged from zero to more than 2,800, with heavy fire activity at a few different locations across the Western United States. Lightning flash densities (fig. 3.3) ranged from zero to 59 flashes km^{-2}, with peak lightning activity in Southern Florida. The low level of lightning activity in West Coast States and in Maine follows a consistent pattern that has been noted previously (Huffines and Orville 1999).

The relationship between lightning flash density and forest fire occurrence in the Eastern United States appears to be different from the relationship between lightning flash density and forest fire occurrence in the Western United States. There was a large, significant positive correlation between lightning flash density and forest fire occurrence ($r = 0.59$, $p<0.0001$) in the Eastern United States. In contrast, there was a statistically significant negative correlation between lightning flash density and forest fire occurrence ($r = -0.20$, $p<0.0001$) in the Western United States. This may not be surprising, as lightning activity is low and fire frequency high in many parts of the Western United States.

Nevertheless, when the data were analyzed at a finer spatial scale, lightning and fire occurrence were positively correlated in most individual ecoregion provinces in the United States, including many in the Western United States (fig. 3.4). There were large and statistically significant positive correlations between lightning and fire occurrence in four densely forested provinces covering much of the Southeastern and Mid-Atlantic United States: 231—Southeastern Mixed Forest ($r = 0.46$, $p<0.0001$); 232—Outer Coastal Plain

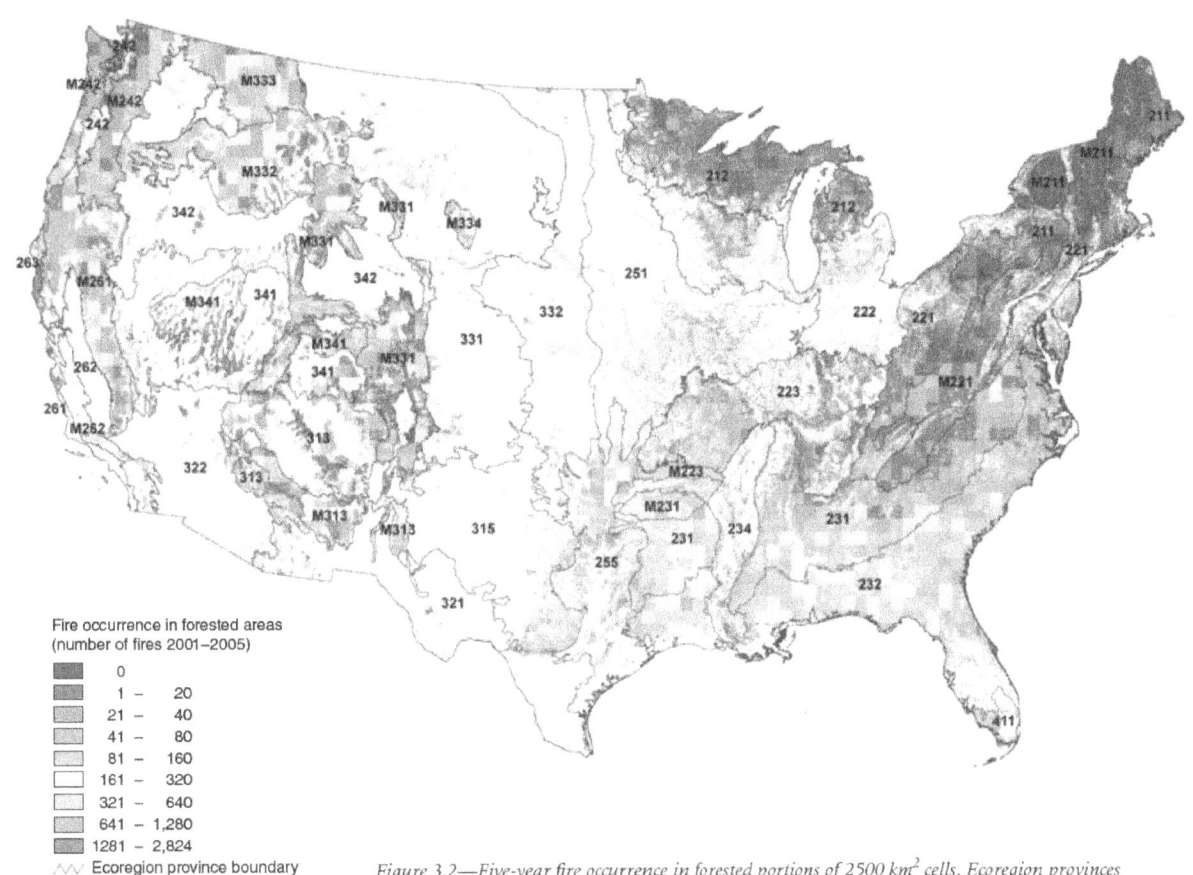

Fire occurrence in forested areas
(number of fires 2001–2005)

- 0
- 1 – 20
- 21 – 40
- 41 – 80
- 81 – 160
- 161 – 320
- 321 – 640
- 641 – 1,280
- 1281 – 2,824
- Ecoregion province boundary

Figure 3.2—Five-year fire occurrence in forested portions of 2500 km² cells. Ecoregion provinces (Cleland and others 2005) are shown for reference. Forest cover source was the U.S. Department of Agriculture Forest Service, Remote Sensing Applications Center. (Data source: U.S. Department of Agriculture, Forest Service, Remote Sensing Applications Center)

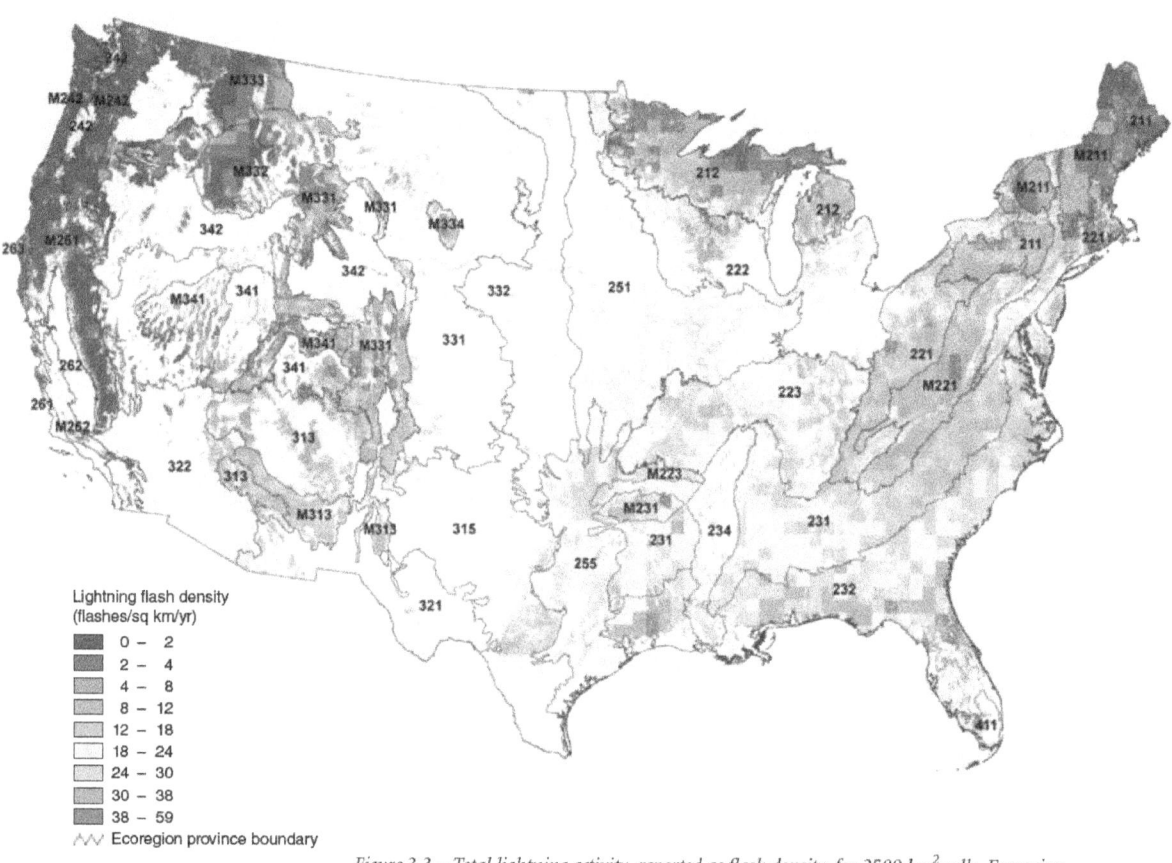

Lightning flash density
(flashes/sq km/yr)

- 0 – 2
- 2 – 4
- 4 – 8
- 8 – 12
- 12 – 18
- 18 – 24
- 24 – 30
- 30 – 38
- 38 – 59

/\/\/ Ecoregion province boundary

Figure 3.3—Total lightning activity, reported as flash density, for 2500 km² cells. Ecoregion provinces (Cleland and others 2005) are shown for reference. Forest cover source was the U.S. Department of Agriculture Forest Service, Remote Sensing Applications Center. [Data source: National Aeronautics and Space Administration Global Hydrology Resource Center]

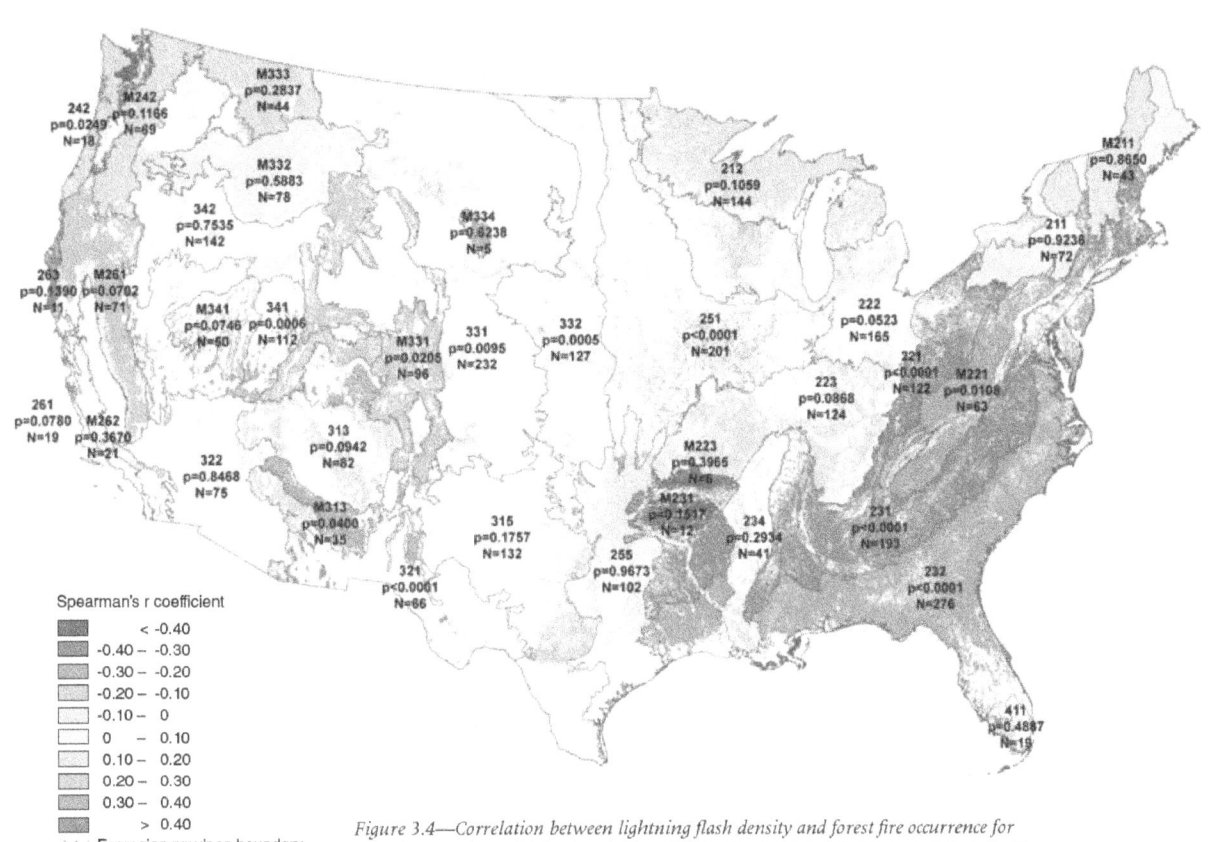

Spearman's r coefficient

- ▨   < -0.40
- ▨   -0.40 – -0.30
- ▨   -0.30 – -0.20
- ▨   -0.20 – -0.10
- ▨   -0.10 – 0
- ☐   0 – 0.10
- ▨   0.10 – 0.20
- ▨   0.20 – 0.30
- ▨   0.30 – 0.40
- ▨   > 0.40

∿∿ Ecoregion province boundary

Figure 3.4—Correlation between lightning flash density and forest fire occurrence for ecoregion provinces (Cleland and others 2005). P-value labels indicate statistical significance of correlation. (Province 262—California Dry Steppe omitted because of limited forested area.) [Data sources: U.S. Department of Agriculture Forest Service, Remote Sensing Applications Center, and National Aeronautics and Space Administration Global Hydrology Resource Center]

Mixed Forest (r = 0.32, p<0.0001); 221—Eastern Broadleaf Forest (r = 0.42, p<0.0001); and M221—Central Appalachian Broadleaf Forest—Coniferous Forest—Meadow (r = 0.32, p = 0.0108) (fig. 3.4). The results for the latter two provinces may be influenced by geography. These northsouth oriented provinces extend hundreds of kilometers across a range of lightning densities, but small areas of high lightning density co-occurred with clusters of forest fire activity in their southern portions.

Two mostly forested provinces in the Western United States also exhibited significant positive correlations: M331—Southern Rocky Mountain Steppe—Open Woodland—Coniferous Forest—Alpine Meadow (r = 0.24, p = 0.0205) and M313—Arizona—New Mexico Mountains Semi-Desert—Open Woodland—Coniferous Forest—Alpine Meadow (r = 0.35, p = 0.04). Elsewhere, significant positive correlation was not restricted to heavily forested areas. Four patchily forested provinces exhibited strong positive correlations: 251—Prairie Parkland (Temperate) (r = 0.32,

p<0.0001); 332—Great Plains Steppe (r = 0.30, p = 0.0005); 321—Chihuahuan Semi-Desert (r = 0.47, p<0.0001); and 341—Intermountain Semi-Desert and Desert (r = 0.32, p = 0.0006). In these provinces, peak lightning flash density values were relatively low compared to those in provinces in the Southeastern United States, but the locations of those peak values coincided with the provinces' mostly densely forested areas and greatest fire activity.

One sparsely forested province in the Great Lakes Region, 222—Midwest Broadleaf Forest, displayed a small negative correlation with borderline statistical significance (r = −0.15, p = 0.0523). Province 331—Great Plains—Palouse Dry Steppe also exhibited a small but significant negative correlation (r = −0.17, p = 0.0095). This province displayed substantial fire activity near the Canadian border, where lightning density was quite low. Ultimately, only one province displayed a large and significant negative correlation between fire and lightning activity, 242—Pacific Lowland Mixed Forest (r = −0.53, p = 0.0249). This, along with a mix of nonsignificant positive and negative correlations in northern Rocky Mountain Provinces, may support Rorig and Ferguson (2002), who argued that dewpoint depression and atmospheric instability are better predictors of lightning-caused fires than total lightning activity for the Northwestern United States because fires in the region are typically ignited only by "dry lightning" (lightning when there is little or no measurable rainfall).

This preliminary analysis ignored several factors that may affect spatio-temporal patterns of forest fire ignitions. For example, the potential importance of atmospheric and climatic conditions for ignition likelihood has already been noted. Also, forest fuel moisture and condition may vary seasonally, and this may affect the likelihood of fire ignition (Rorig and Ferguson 2002). Moreover, this analysis disregarded fuel type and current fire regime, both of which may vary at multiple spatial scales (Morgan and others 2001, Rorig and Ferguson 2002). Before drawing any conclusions, it is important to consider that in many parts of the Eastern United States, and especially in the Northeast, lightning has historically caused fewer wildland fires than have anthropogenic ignitions (Stephens 2005). However, anthropogenic fires are typically small compared to lightning-caused fires (Larjavaara and others 2005), and are more likely to be extinguished quickly, so the MODIS fire occurrence data are unlikely to depict most of them. Ideally, the forest cover masking process used to filter the occurrence data for this analysis tended to favor larger, lightning-caused fires in sizeable forested areas, but it is currently impossible to determine for any given region what proportion of the remaining MODIS forest fire occurrences are actually lightning-caused. It may also be true that the spatial pattern of human-related fire activity correlates with the spatial pattern of lightning activity. Irrespective of ignition source or other confounding effects, the results suggest that lightning flash density can serve as a useful general predictor of where fires are likely to occur for forested areas in the Eastern United States. However, it may also be advisable to include human population density in any predictive model. Four eastern provinces exhibited sizeable, statistically significant negative correlations between population density and forest fire occurrence: 231—Southeastern Mixed Forest (r = –0.50, p<0.0001); 232—Outer Coastal Plain Mixed Forest (r = –0.39, p<0.0001); 221—Eastern Broadleaf Forest (r = –0.40, p<0.0001); and M221—Central Appalachian Broadleaf Forest— Coniferous Forest—Meadow (r = –0.33, p = 0.0108). Notably, these same provinces exhibited large positive correlations between lightning flash density and fire occurrence. A succinct explanation of the negative correlations is that forest fires are likely to occur in the most heavily forested areas, where the human population density logically tends to be low. In any case, population density appears to be at least as important as lightning density in explaining forest fire pattern in much of the Eastern United States.

Success of lightning flash density as a predictor appears mixed for the Western United States, although there are certain ecoregion provinces, particularly in the Southwest, where the relationship between lightning and forest fire occurrence appears quite strong. Most western provinces did not exhibit correlations with population density, although three patchily forested ecoregion provinces in the West exhibited significant positive correlations between population density and forest fire occurrence: 332—Great Plains Steppe (r = 0.34, p = 0.0001); 321—Chihuahuan Semi-Desert (r = 0.28, p<0.0251); and 341—Intermountain Semi-Desert and Desert (r = 0.38, p<0.0001). This may be partially explained by the tendency of these provinces to exhibit high population densities in those areas where the limited amount of forest is also concentrated. Nevertheless, given the recent history of drought in several Western U.S. provinces (see chapter 2, "Drought," in this report), timely analyses that apply lightning density as an explanatory variable in conjunction with other relevant factors, e.g., forest fuel spatial pattern, historic fire regime, might provide information that could be used to reduce forest fire risk in these areas in the near future.

Literature Cited

Boccippio, D.J.; Cummins, K.L.; Christian, H.J.; Goodman, S.J. 2001. Combined satellite- and surface-based estimation of the intracloud-cloud-to-ground lightning ratio over the continental United States. Monthly Weather Review. 129: 108–122.

Cleland, D.T.; Freeouf, J.A.; Keys, J.E. [and others]. 2005. Ecological subregions: sections and subsections for the conterminous United States. Washington, DC: U.S. Department of Agriculture Forest Service. [Map, presentation scale 1:3,500,000; colored]. [Also on CD–ROM as a Geographic Information System coverage in ArcINFO format].

Environmental Systems Research Institute. 2006. ESRI data and maps 2006 [CD–ROM]. Redlands, CA: Environmental Systems Research Institute. Giglio, L.; Descloitres, J.; Justice, C.O.; Kaufman, Y. 2003. An enhanced contextual fire detection algorithm for MODIS. Remote Sensing of Environment. 87: 273–282.

Huffines, G.R.; Orville, R.E. 1999. Lightning ground flash density and thunderstorm duration in the continental United States. Journal of Applied Meteorology. 38: 1013–1019.

Larjavaara, M.; Pennanen, J.; Tuomi, T.J. 2005. Lightning that ignites forest fires in Finland. Agricultural and Forest Meteorology. 132: 171–180.

Morgan, P.; Hardy, C.C.; Swetnam, T.W. [and others]. 2001. Mapping fire regimes across time and space: understanding coarse and fine-scale fire patterns. International Journal of Wildland Fire. 10: 329–342.

National Aeronautics and Space Administration. 2006. MODIS Web site. http://modis.gsfc.nasa.gov/. [Date accessed: May 22].

National Aeronautics and Space Administration, Global Hydrology Resource Center. 2004. LIS/OTD 0.5-degree high resolution full climatology. http://ghrc.msfc.nasa.gov/. [Date accessed: March 7, 2006].

Rorig, M.L.; Ferguson, S. 1999. Characteristics of lightning and wildland fire ignition in the Pacific Northwest. Journal of Applied Meteorology. 38: 1565–1575.

Rorig, M.L.; Ferguson, S. 2002. The 2000 fire season: lightning-caused fires. Journal of Applied Meteorology. 41: 786–791.

Rykiel, E.J.; Coulson, R.N.; Sharpe, P.J.H. [and others] 1988. Disturbance propagation by bark beetles as an episodic landscape phenomenon. Landscape Ecology. 1(3): 129–139.

SAS Institute Inc. 1999. SAS/STAT user's guide. Version 8. Cary, NC. 3,884 p.

Steel, R.G.D.; Torrie, J.H.; Dickey, D.A. 1997. Principles and procedures of statistics, a iometrical approach. 3^d ed. United States: The McGraw-Hill Companies. 666 p.

Stephens, S.L. 2005. Forest fire causes and extent on United States Forest Service lands. International Journal of Wildland Fire. 14(3): 213–222.

U.S. Department of Agriculture Forest Service, Remote Sensing Applications Center. 2006. MODIS active fire mapping program: GIS data. http://activefiremaps.fs.fed.us/fireptdata.php. [Date accessed: March 21].

Vasquez, A.; Moreno, J.M. 1998. Patterns of lightning-, and people-caused fires in peninsular Spain. International Journal of Wildland Fire. 8(2): 103–115.

Zajac, B.A.; Rutledge, S.A. 2001. Cloud-to-ground lightning activity in the contiguous United States from 1995 to 1999. Monthly Weather Review. 129: 999–1019.

The influence of air pollutants on ecosystems in the United States is an important environmental issue. The term "air pollution" encompasses a wide range of topics, but acid deposition and ozone are primary concerns in the context of forest health. Acid deposition partially results from emissions of sulfur dioxide, nitrogen oxides, and ammonia that are deposited in wet form as sulfate (SO_4^{2-}), nitrate (NO_3^-), and ammonium (NH_4^+) by rain, snow, and sleet. Inputs of sulfur and nitrogen can also come from dry deposition or from clouds and fog (Driscoll and others 2001). Tropospheric ozone develops during photochemical reactions between nitrogen oxides and volatile organic compounds. Acid deposition can affect soil and water acidity (Driscoll and others 2001), and ozone can cause foliar injury (Chappelka and Samuelson 1998, Cleveland and Graedel 1979, Lefohn and Pinkerton 1988). However, dose-response relationships are complicated and depend heavily on species composition, edaphic factors, and climatic conditions.

Fenn and others (2003) provided a generalized comparison between air pollution in the Eastern and Western United States. In the East, sulfur deposition has been higher than nitrogen deposition and wet deposition is predominant. However, there is evidence that sulfur deposition has decreased. In the West, dry nitrogen deposition dominates. In the East, atmospheric pollution is considered a regional issue; in the West, where deposition rates decline quickly with increased distance from the pollutant source areas, this is not the case. In the West, ozone causes the most severe injury to forests. However, this mostly occurs in California in combination with nitrogen deposition. In the East, ozone causes injury to sensitive species in some areas, and nitrogen and sulfur deposition may be important factors in declining tree growth in some areas.

Chapter 4. Air Pollution: Tropospheric Ozone, and Wet Deposition of Sulfate and Inorganic Nitrogen

John W. Coulston

Brief Methods

For the purposes of this report I examined wet inorganic nitrogen and sulfate deposition from 2000 through 2004, and ozone exposure for the same period. Inorganic nitrogen is total nitrogen in wet nitrate (NO_3^-) and wet ammonium (NH_4^+) deposition. Annual wet deposition summaries were acquired from the National Atmospheric Deposition Program (NADP) (http://nadp.sws.uiuc.edu/). Daily ambient ozone concentrations were acquired from the U.S. Environmental Protection Agency (EPA) Air Quality System (http://www.epa.gov/ttn/airs/airsaqs/index.htm). Annual 3-month growing season, 12-hour SUM06 ozone summaries were calculated based on suggestions provided by the EPA (2004). The SUM06 ozone index is the sum of all hourly concentrations > 0.06 parts per million (ppm), and I consider June, July, and August the 3-month growing season. The standard units for SUM06 are ppm-hours. The approach suggested by Coulston and others (2004) was used to estimate the status and trends in exposure of forests to ozone,

wet sulfate deposition, and wet deposition of nitrogen. This technique uses the linear model $D = a+b(y)$, where D is the weighted average deposition value, b is the weighted average annual change, and y is year. The probability that $b = 0$ was tested with an F-test and significance was assigned at the 0.05 level. For display purposes, interpolated surfaces of each pollutant were created using gradient plus inverse distance squared interpolation (Nalder and Wein 1998). The accuracy of each surface was examined by calculating the root mean square error.

Results

There was a strong east-west gradient in average annual (2000–04) wet sulfate and wet inorganic nitrogen deposition amounts in the conterminous United States. Wet sulfate deposition was highest in the Northeast Forest Health Monitoring (FHM) region from 2000 through 2004 (fig. 4.1). On average, forests in the Northeast FHM region received approximately 17.6 kg ha^{-1} per year of wet

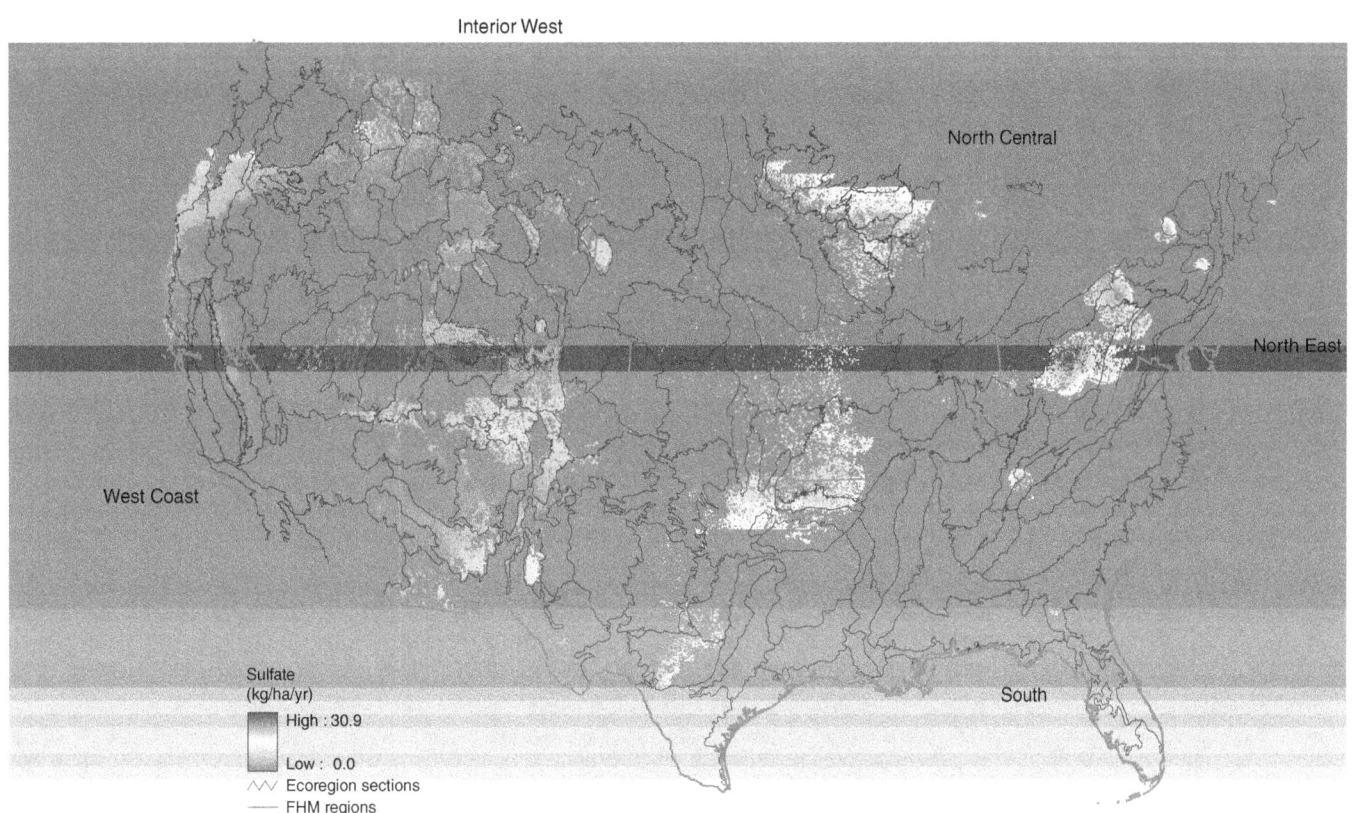

Interior West

North Central

North East

West Coast

South

Sulfate
(kg/ha/yr)

High : 30.9

Low : 0.0

∧∧∧ Ecoregion sections

—— FHM regions

Figure 4.1—Mean wet sulfate deposition for forested areas from 2000 through 2004. The average root mean square error of the interpolation was approximately 2.67 kg ha⁻¹ per year based on cross-validation. Ecoregion sections (Cleland and others 2005) are shown for reference. (Data source: National Atmospheric Deposition Program)

sulfate deposition annually during the time period (table 4.1). Wet inorganic nitrogen deposition was highest in the North Central FHM region, where forests received on average 5.13 kg ha^{-1} per year from 2000 through 2004 (fig. 4.2, table 4.1). Wet inorganic nitrogen deposition in the Northeast FHM region was similar, at 5.01 kg ha^{-1} per year. For the period 2000–04, forested areas in the Interior West FHM region had the lowest average annual wet sulfate deposition rate (1.65 kg ha^{-1} per year) and forested areas in the West Coast FHM region had the lowest wet inorganic nitrogen deposition rate (1.04 kg ha^{-1} per year) (table 4.1).

From 2000 through 2004 in the conterminous United States, wet deposition exposure rates to forests were relatively constant. Over that period, forests in most FHM regions had average annual changes in wet deposition of sulfate and of inorganic nitrogen that did not significantly differ from 0 kg ha^{-1} per year per year at the p<0.05 level (table 4.1). Forests in the South FHM region were the exception. They experienced a statistically significant (p<0.05) increase in wet inorganic nitrogen deposition (0.17 kg ha^{-1} per year per year) over the period (table 4.1).

Table 4.1—Average and average annual change of forest exposure to wet inorganic nitrogen deposition, wet sulfate deposition, and SUM06 ozone from 2000 through 2004 by FHM region

FHM region	Inorganic N		SO$_4$$^{2-}$		SUM06	
	Average	Average annual change	Average	Average annual change	Average	Average annual change
	kg ha^{-1} yr^{-1}	kg ha^{-1} yr^{-2}	kg ha^{-1} yr^{-1}	kg ha^{-1} yr^{-2}	ppm-hrs yr^{-1}	ppm-hrs yr^{-2}
Interior West	1.23	0.05	1.65	0	18.37	-1.04[a]
North Central	5.13	-0.11	10.13	-0.15	9.46	-0.85[a]
North East	5.01	-0.02	17.6	0.19	13.64	-0.86[a]
South	4.1	0.17[a]	13.75	0.28	15.84	-3.97[a]
West Coast	1.04	0	2.23	-0.08	13.09	0.53

[a] Indicates statistical significance at P<0.05.

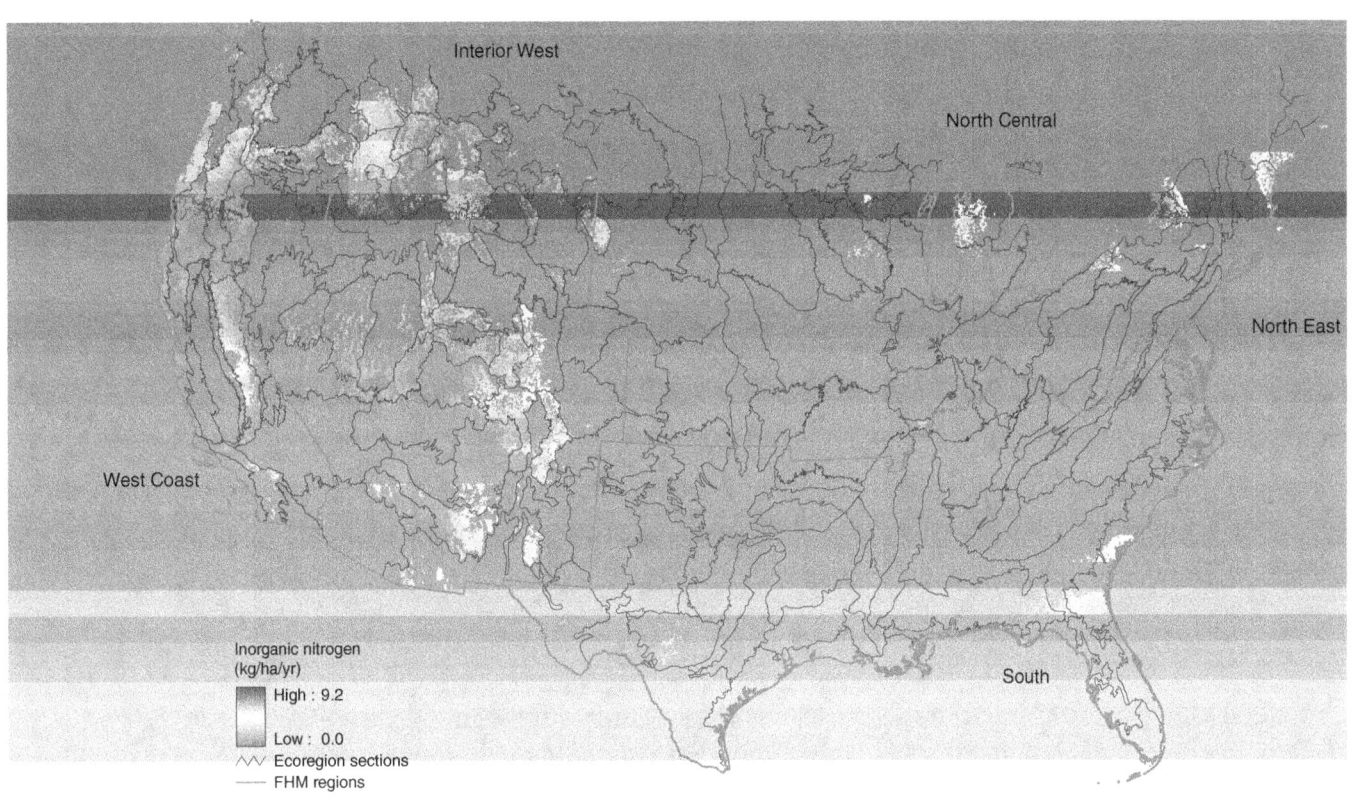

Interior West

North Central

North East

West Coast

South

Inorganic nitrogen
(kg/ha/yr)

High : 9.2

Low : 0.0
∧∧∧ Ecoregion sections
—— FHM regions

Figure 4.2—Mean wet inorganic nitrogen deposition for forested areas from 2000 through 2004. The average root mean square error of the interpolation was approximately 0.87 kg ha^{-1} per year based on cross-validation. Ecoregion sections (Cleland and others 2005) are shown for reference. (Data source: National Atmospheric Deposition Program)

31

Average annual (2000–04) ambient 3-month growing-season SUM06 ozone exposures in some portion of the forested areas exceeded 20 ppm-hours per year in all FHM regions (fig. 4.3). Average exposure was highest in forests in the Interior West FHM region (18.4 ppm-hours per year) (table 4.1). In the West Coast FHM region the average exposure was 13.1 ppm-hours per year for the period 2000–04. However, this region had both forests with the highest exposures, e.g., section M261E—Sierra Nevada in California, and forests with very low exposures, e.g., section M242D—Northern Cascades in Washington. In the Eastern United States, forests in the South FHM region had ozone exposure that averaged 15.8 ppm-hours per year, but there was a statistically significant decreasing trend ($p<0.05$) of 3.97 ppm-hours per year per year from 2000 through 2004 (table 4.1). Forests in the Interior West, North Central, and Northeast FHM regions also had statistically decreasing trends in ozone exposure of 1.04 ppm-hours per year, 0.85 ppm-hours per year per year, and 0.86 ppm-hours per year per year, respectively (table 4.1).

Discussion

There is a complex air pollution dose-response relationship in forests. In the case of wet sulfate and inorganic nitrogen deposition, factors such as watershed bedrock composition, land use history, vegetation type, soil depth, and the ability of the soil to neutralize acidic inputs partly determine whether the input will result in a response such as soil acidification (Ecological Society of America 2000). The influence of ambient ozone concentrations on vegetation depends on climatic conditions and species composition.

The EPA (2002) described the following forest-type groups as sensitive to and subject to high deposition rates: high-elevation spruce/fir, southern pine and pine/hardwood, eastern hardwoods in the Great Lakes area, the Colorado alpine meadow, western conifers, and southern California urban forests. The analysis presented here did not identify "high" wet deposition rates in the Western United States. However, estimates of dry deposition were not included, and according to Fenn and others (2003) dry deposition is an important source of nitrogen input. Also, this analysis did not take any information about soil or vegetation type into account. The results only relate to inputs to forest ecosystems.

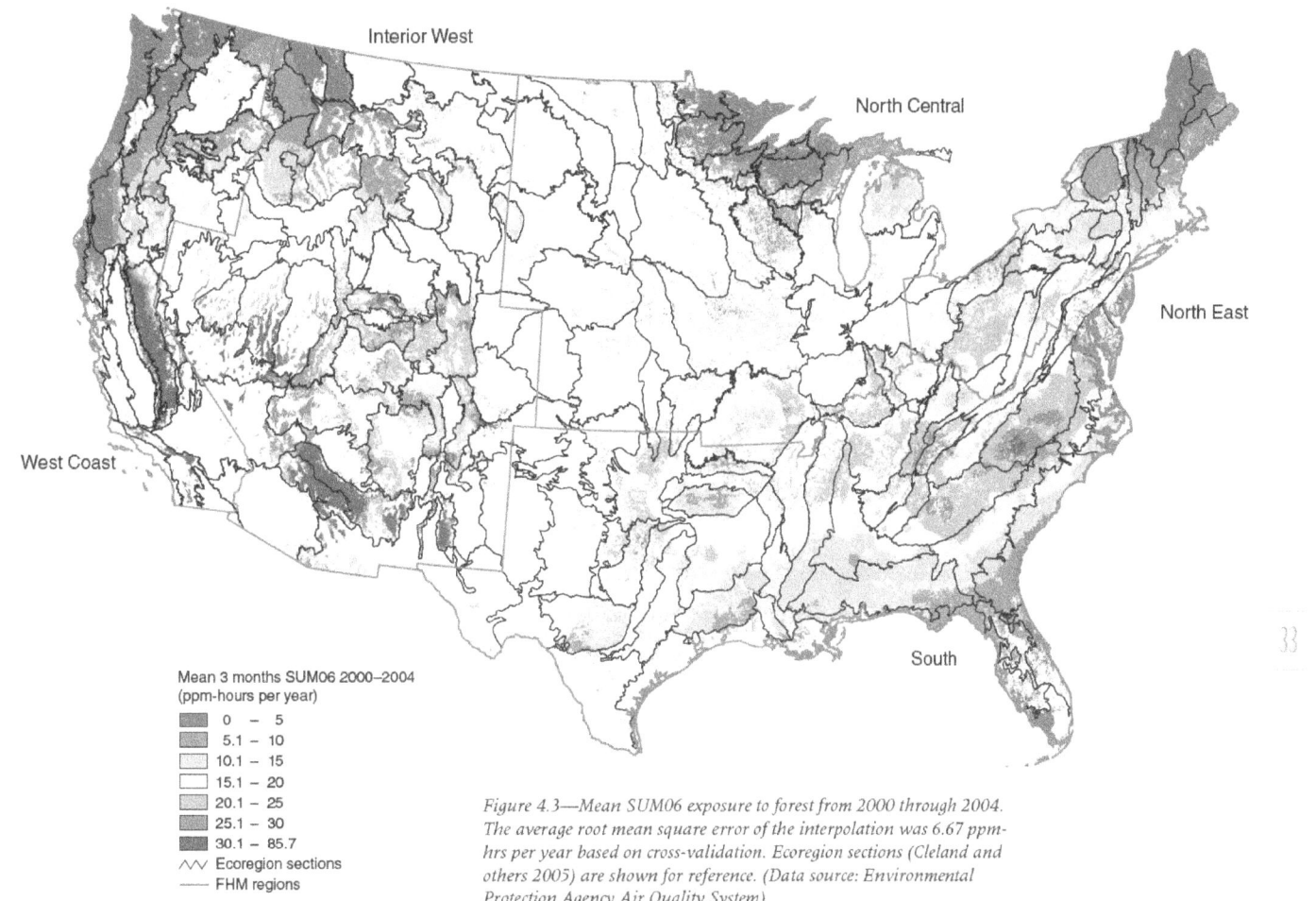

Interior West

North Central

North East

West Coast

South

Mean 3 months SUM06 2000–2004
(ppm-hours per year)

0 – 5
5.1 – 10
10.1 – 15
15.1 – 20
20.1 – 25
25.1 – 30
30.1 – 85.7
∧∧∨ Ecoregion sections
—— FHM regions

Figure 4.3—Mean SUM06 exposure to forest from 2000 through 2004. The average root mean square error of the interpolation was 6.67 ppm-hrs per year based on cross-validation. Ecoregion sections (Cleland and others 2005) are shown for reference. (Data source: Environmental Protection Agency Air Quality System)

Literature Cited

Chappelka, A.H.; Samuelson, L.J. 1998. Ambient ozone effects on forest trees of the Eastern United States: a review. New Phytologist. 139(1): 91–108.

Cleland, D.T.; Freeouf, J.A.; Keys, J.E. [and others]. 2005. Ecological subregions: sections and subsections for the conterminous United States. Washington, DC: U.S. Department of Agriculture Forest Service. [Map, presentation scale 1:3,500,000; colored]. [Also on CD–ROM as a Geographic Information System coverage in ArcINFO format].

Cleveland, W.S.; Graedel, T.E. 1979. Photochemical air pollution in the Northeast United States. Science. 204: 1273–1278.

Coulston, J.W.; Riitters, K.H.; Smith, G.C. 2004. A preliminary assessment of Montreal process indicators of air pollution for the United States. Environmental Monitoring and Assessment. 95: 57–74.

Driscoll, C.T.; Lawrence, G.B.; Bulger, A.J. [and others]. 2001. Acid deposition in the Northeastern United States: sources and inputs, ecosystem effects, and management strategies. BioScience. 51(3): 180–198.

Ecological Society of America. 2000. Acid deposition. Available online: http://www.esa.org/education/edupdfs/aciddeposition.pdf. [Date accessed: June 13, 2006].

Fenn, M.E.; Baron, J.S.; Allen, E.B. [and others]. 2003. Ecological effects of nitrogen deposition in the Western United States. BioScience. 53(4): 404–420.

Lefohn, A.S.; Pinkerton, J.E. 1988. High resolution characterization of ozone data for sites located in forested areas of the United States. Journal of the Air Pollution Control Association. 38: 1504–1511.

Nalder, I.A.; Wein, R.W. 1998. Spatial interpolation of climatic normals: test of a new method in the Canadian boreal forest. Agricultural and Forest Meteorology. 92(4): 211–225.

U.S. Environmental Protection Agency. 2002. Nitrogen: multiple and regional impacts. EPA–430–R–01–006. Washington, DC: U.S. Environmental Protection Agency, Clean Air Markets Division. 38 p.

U.S. Environmental Protection Agency. 2004. Air quality system raw data summarization formulas. Draft version 1.1. Available online: http://www.epa.gov/ttn/airs/airsaqs/manuals/Precision%20and%20Accuracy%20Summary%20Formulas.pdf. [Date accessed: June 13, 2006].

Why Are Epiphytic Lichen Communities Important?

L ichens are one of the bioindicators used by the Forest Inventory and Analysis (FIA) Program to monitor forest health. To obtain data for use in its Lichen Community Indicator Program, FIA samples a regular network of permanent field plots to determine the composition of epiphytic, i.e., tree dwelling, lichen communities. The FIA lichens dataset is an important reservoir of information with many potential biomonitoring applications. The composition of a lichen community reflects various aspects of the local forest environment such as stand age, disturbance history, local climate, and stand structure. Perhaps the best known and most tested application of the Lichen Community Indicator data, however, is its utility for describing and monitoring air quality.

Many lichens are extremely sensitive to environmental change and are expected to be adversely affected by stressors such as air pollution before the rest of the ecosystem. Lichen community responses to various forms of both nitrogen (N) and sulfur (S) pollutants are well documented (e.g., Gauslaa 1995, Hawksworth and Rose 1970, Jovan and McCune 2005, McCune 1988, van Herk 1999), while responses to ozone are currently under investigation (Jovan and McCune 2005, Nash and Sigal 1999, Ruoss and Vonarburg 1995). The main purpose of this chapter is to provide an overview of potential air quality impacts on forest health in western Oregon and Washington as identified by the FIA Lichen Community Indicator Program. Baseline FIA results are reported together with a review of major findings from a related air quality study conducted by Geiser and Neitlich (2007).

Methods

Field methods—Members of each FIA field crew are trained and certified to conduct time-constrained lichen community surveys at FIA phase 3 plots (U.S. Department of Agriculture Forest Service 2006). These surveys last between 30 minutes and 2 hours, and during this time the abundance of each epiphytic species encountered is estimated using a broad abundance code (table 5.1). A voucher specimen is collected for each species and later identified by a lichen specialist in the lab. All material

Chapter 5. Baseline Results from the Lichen Community Indicator Program in the Pacific Northwest: Air Quality Patterns and Evidence of a Nitrogen Pollution Problem

Sarah Jovan

Table 5.1—Abundance codes used during lichen community surveys

Code	Abundance
1	Rare (1–3 thalli[a])
2	Uncommon (4–10 thalli[a])
3	Common (>10 thalli[a]; species occurring on < 50 percent of all boles and branches in plot)
4	Abundant (>10 thalli[a]; species occurring on > 50 percent of boles and branches in plot)

[a] A thallus is the body of the lichen. Hence, "thalli," as used here, refers to the number of individuals.

is collected without the aid of ladders or tree climbing. Crew performance is audited by means of hot checks, in which specialists and crews survey simultaneously, or by means of blind checks, in which specialists resurvey plots within 2 months of the crew survey. Crews must capture at least 65 percent of the species found by the specialist, as this level of agreement has been shown to yield repeatable air quality estimates across observers (McCune and others 1997).

Model building and application—Analysts use the lichen community data to build gradient models with statistical tools such as regression and nonmetric multidimensional scaling ordination (NMS) (Kruskal 1964, McCune and Grace 2002). NMS models are the norm for lichen gradient modeling and provide estimates of both air quality and local forest climate. Basically, NMS analysis determines how the species composition of each plot differs from that of every other plot using a quantitative descriptor called a distance measure. This descriptor helps NMS detect gradients in lichen community composition and order plots along them. This ordering of plots in terms of lichen community is then related to environmental gradients. For instance, an air quality gradient across the landscape is often reflected by a detectable change in lichen community composition wherein certain indicator species increase in abundance while others decrease. Each plot gets a score along the community gradient, which serves as an estimate of relative air quality.

Geiser and Neitlich (2007), in collaboration with FIA and the Forest Service Region 6 Air Resource Program, developed an NMS model for biomonitoring air quality in Pacific Northwest (PNW) forests west of the Cascades crest (fig. 5.1). In this parent study, the model was applied to survey data from over 1,500 plots including FIA phase 3 plots, hundreds of sites on the Forest Service Region 6 Current Vegetation Survey grid (Max and others 1996), and "off-frame" sites in areas of special interest such as urban forests, wilderness areas, and forest stands near air quality monitors.

Ideally, direct measurements of air pollution concentrations are used to help calibrate NMS lichen models. Air quality monitoring station coverage was insufficient, so Geiser and Neitlich (2007) supplemented most community surveys with collection of lichens for chemical analysis. Lichens accumulate airborne chemicals, and elemental concentrations in the lichen are indicative of local deposition (Bruteig 1993, Geiser 2004, Søchting 1995).

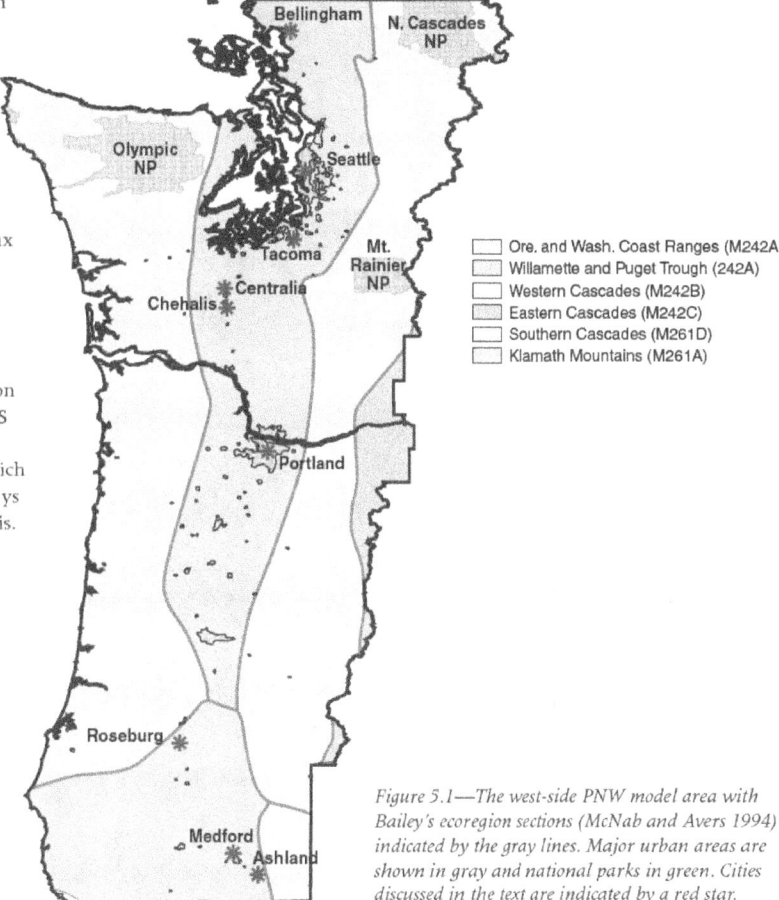

Ore. and Wash. Coast Ranges (M242A)
Willamette and Puget Trough (242A)
Western Cascades (M242B)
Eastern Cascades (M242C)
Southern Cascades (M261D)
Klamath Mountains (M261A)

Figure 5.1—The west-side PNW model area with Bailey's ecoregion sections (McNab and Avers 1994) indicated by the gray lines. Major urban areas are shown in gray and national parks in green. Cities discussed in the text are indicated by a red star.

For the following summary, the NMS model was applied to data from 243 plots sampled for lichens between 1998–2001 or 2003, which constitute a full cycle of FIA survey data. Results are integrated with highlights from the research of Geiser and Neitlich (2007). Data for about 75 percent of FIA plots were included in the extensive analytical dataset analyzed by Geiser and Neitlich. Sites surveyed on the FIA phase 3 grid provide an unbiased, systematic sample of conditions across the forested landscape and serve as the official basis for comparison. Eleven of the 243 FIA phase 3 lichen plots also were included among 293 plots in the calibration dataset used by Geiser and Neitlich (2007) to develop the model.

What Do the Data Show?

Is nitrogen the culprit?—The data analyzed by Geiser and Neitlich (2007) contained strong evidence that nitrogen (N) pollution, in particular, is a major contributor to air quality degradation in western Oregon and Washington.

The first clue lies in the N content of lichens, which served as the strongest predictor of air quality scores ($r^2 = 0.53$) reported by Geiser and Neitlich (2007); plots with high scores tended to have lichens with high N. A map of N in lichens can be found in Fenn and others (2003a).

A second clue is the prominence of certain species at high-scoring sites that are indicators of N-rich conditions. These lichens, known as the "nitrophytes" (fig. 5.2), are currently used to help detect where elevated N inputs are reaching forests in California (Jovan and McCune 2005, 2006). Characterization of nitrophyte populations similarly forms the backbone of numerous European N-biomonitoring programs (Lambley and Wolseley 2004).

The positive association between nitrophytes and high gradient model scores is simply illustrated by overlaying a nitrophytic species' abundance on plot coordinates from the NMS model (fig. 5.3). This basic relationship is likewise demonstrated statistically by Geiser

Figure 5.2—Physcia adscendens, *a common nitrophytic lichen (top), and pollution-sensitive* Lobaria oregana *(bottom). Photos courtesy of Sarah Jovan (top) and Eric Straley (bottom).*

and Neitlich (2007). They used indicator species analysis (ISA) (Dufrêne and Legendre 1997) to determine that three classically nitrophytic species (*Candelaria concolor*, *Physcia adscendens*, and *Xanthoria polycarpa*) were the strongest indicators of plots with the highest scores. "Strong indicators" as defined by ISA in this case technically means that these species are consistently present in high-scoring plots, but uncommon in plots with low air scores (McCune and Grace 2002). From a community perspective, however, nitrophyte enhancement is only half the story. Several species exhibit a

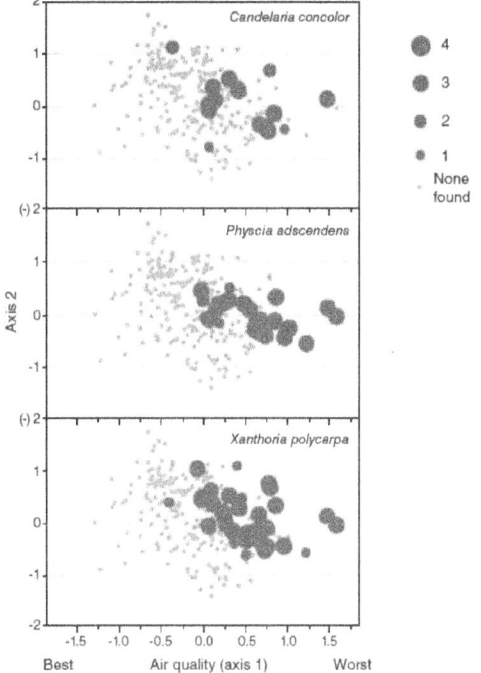

Figure 5.3—Abundance codes (table 5.1) for the three strongest indicator species of polluted plots (Geiser and Neitlich 2007) overlaid on plot scores. Plot scores for the two gradients in the nonmetric multidimensional scaling ordination model are represented by plot coordinates on the two axes in the diagram. Axis 1 represents the air quality gradient, while axis 2 represents a climatic gradient (not discussed here; see Geiser and Neitlich 2007). Plots where each species was absent are tan. Otherwise, symbol size indicates abundance code. (Additional data source: U.S. Department of Agriculture Forest Service, FIA Program)

marked negative association with the air quality gradient (fig. 5.4). Examples include the well-known sensitive species *Bryoria capillaris*, *Lobaria oregana* (fig. 5.2), and *Sphaerophorus globosus*, which Geiser and Neitlich (2007) determined to be among the strongest indicators of the "cleanest" sites (fig. 5.4).

Geographic distribution—Air quality scores for FIA plots are summarized in figure 5.5 and table 5.2 using six "air quality zones" devised by Geiser and Neitlich (2007): best, good, fair, degraded, poor, and worst. Zones are based on the distribution of air quality scores for

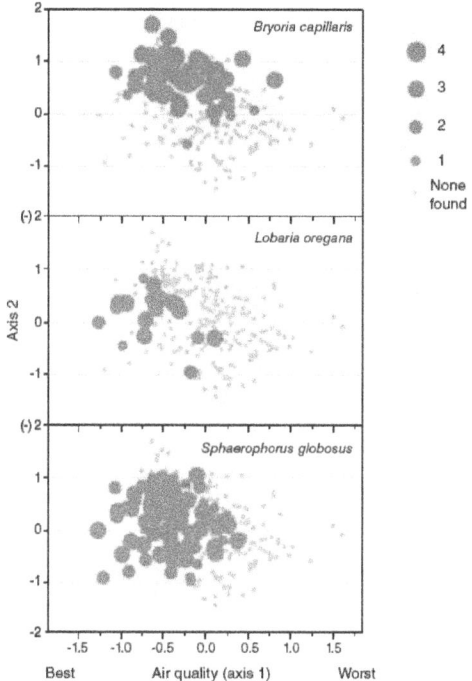

Figure 5.4—Abundance codes (table 5.1) for the three species that are strongest indicators of clean air (pollution-sensitive species) (Geiser and Neitlich 2007) overlaid on plot scores. Plot scores for the two gradients in the nonmetric multidimensional scaling ordination model are represented by plot coordinates on the two axes in the diagram. Axis 1 represents the air quality gradient, while axis 2 represents a climatic gradient (not discussed here; please see Geiser and Neitlich 2007). Plots where species was absent are blue. Otherwise, symbol size indicates abundance code. (Additional data source: U.S. Department of Agriculture Forest Service, FIA Program)

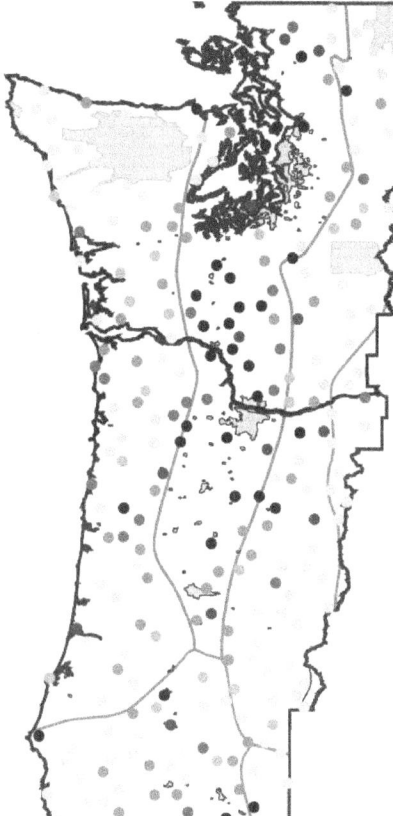

Best (-1.4 to -0.11)
Good (-0.11 to -0.02)
Fair (-0.02 to 0.21)
Degraded (0.21 to 0.35)
Poor (0.35 to 0.49)
Worst (0.49 to 2.0)

Figure 5.5—Map of air quality scores for all FIA plots (1998–2001, 2003) based on the gradient model of Geiser and Neitlich (2007). Scores are divided into air quality zones signified by colors. The higher the score, the poorer the air quality. Plot locations are approximate. (Data source: U.S. Department of Agriculture Forest Service, FIA Program)

Table 5.2—Summary of FIA plots by ecoregion section and air quality zone

Ecoregion section	Total plots	Best	Good	Fair	Degraded	Poor	Worst
				no.			
M242C—Eastern Cascades	11	10	0	0	1	0	0
M261A—Klamath Mountains	39	18	3	11	3	1	3
M242A—Ore. and Wash. Coast Ranges	70	34	9	15	8	2	2
M261D—Southern Cascades	6	3	0	0	0	1	2
M242B—Western Cascades	64	40	7	9	2	3	3
242A—Willamette Valley and Puget Trough	53	6	1	11	7	6	22
Total	243	111	20	46	21	13	32

FIA = Forest Inventory and Analysis.
Source: Geiser and Neitlich (2007).

plots inhabited by the ISA-derived indicator species. Upper bounds of the best, good, and fair zones are based on the 75th, 90th, and 97.5[th] percentiles of scores associated with the clean air indicators. For example, 75 percent of plots hosting the clean air indicator species had air quality scores <0.11, which serves as the upper bound of the "best" zone (as well as the lower bound of the "good" zone). The upper bound of the "degraded" zone is the 25th percentile of the air quality scores for plots hosting the pollution indicators, while the upper bound of the "poor" zone corresponds to the 100th percentile for clean air indicators. Thus, by definition, none of these sensitive species were present in "worst" plots.

FIA plots in the "worst" air zone were predominantly clustered in ecoregion section 242A—Willamette Valley and Puget Trough [approximately 69 percent of plots in this category (fig. 5.5, table 5.2)]. Many of these sites were associated with large urban areas, e.g., greater Portland metropolitan area, Seattle, Tacoma; as well as smaller cities lining the Interstate 5 corridor, e.g., Bellingham, Chehalis, and Centralia, WA. More remote forests sampled on the periphery of the Willamette Valley, in the eastern Oregon Coast Range, and at low elevations in the Western Cascades, likewise tended to score as "degraded" or worse. Pollution impacts were also detected in forests farther south, in the vicinity of Roseburg, Medford, and Ashland, OR. Geiser and Neitlich (2007) observed the same major hotspots of degradation. Poorly scoring sites on the immediate coast were widely scattered (fig. 5.5), and Geiser and Neitlich (2007) attributed their distribution to local occurrence of pollution point sources and in some cases, the influence of marine aerosols. Few of the FIA sites that were surveyed were within the boundaries of national parks, but sites that were close to national parks were mostly in the "best" category (fig. 5.5). Best scoring sites were located mainly in remote parts (usually midhigh elevation or interior forests) of the Olympic, Cascades, Klamath, and Coast Ranges.

Prognosis

Several ecologically important pollutants are emitted in western Oregon and Washington (Eilers and others 1994, Geiser and Neitlich 2007, Oregon Department of Environmental Quality 2005) and multiple compounds may be influencing lichen communities in that area. However, it is clear that one or more N compounds are primary factors driving the observed patterns. As would be expected, poor scores were common for stands near agricultural and urbanized areas where one finds the most important anthropogenic sources of N, i.e., animal husbandry, fertilizers, and combustion of fossil fuels (Fenn and others 2003b).

N appears to have a major role in shaping the lichen communities farther south in the largely agricultural central valley and surrounding ecosystems, i.e., central coast and Sierra Nevada foothills, in California (Jovan and McCune 2005, 2006). Deposition in western Oregon and Washington appears less severe overall (Bytnerowicz and Fenn 1996, Fenn and others 2003b), although results from the lichen indicator suggest some forests have begun on a trajectory of N enrichment. Currently, forests within and near the 242A—Willamette and Puget Trough ecoregion section seem to be at greatest risk of N impacts (fig. 5.5, table 5.2) (Geiser and Neitlich 2007).

The relatively recent discovery of altered N cycling in some Western U.S. forests has invigorated efforts to monitor deposition and its ecological impact (Baron and others 2000; Fenn and others 1996, 2003a). As most forests in the PNW are naturally adapted to a limited N supply, fertilization can profoundly affect forest function and the quality of associated aquatic systems (Aber and others 1989, Fenn and others 2003a). It is difficult to anticipate ecological impacts of current N levels, however, because critical loads have yet to be identified for most terrestrial systems in the PNW and susceptibility varies widely as a function of numerous biotic and abiotic factors (Porter and others 2005).

Moreover, total N deposition for western ecosystems is largely unknown because patterns in dry N deposition are heterogeneous and poorly characterized (Fenn and others 2003b, Porter and others 2005). While wet deposition is generally low, (see chapter 4) dry N deposition is a major contributor to total N deposition in the Western United States (see chapter 4; Fenn and others 2003a). The bioindication study of Geiser and Neitlich (2007) actually provides the most comprehensive information on N patterns in the region.

The most N-sensitive biological components of western ecosystems, including lichen, fungi, and some plant communities, may be altered by total N deposition as low as 3 to 8 kg N per year (Fenn and others 2003a). From a lichenological standpoint, continued eutrophication in western Oregon and Washington is expected to lead to further dominance by nitrophytes, which possess many of the traits traditionally regarded as "weedy," characteristics that would allow them quickly to establish and dominate a community when conditions are suitable. There would likely be a parallel reduction in ecologically important species like cyanolichens, e.g., *Lobaria*

oregana, (fig. 5.2) and species utilized as forage by wildlife, e.g., *Bryoria* spp., which are among the most pollution sensitive (Fenn and others 2003a). These trends will be tracked closely as additional cycles of data are collected by FIA and the Region 6 Air Resource Program.

Literature Cited

Aber, J.D.; Nadelhoffer, K.J.; Steudler, P.; Melillo, J.M. 1989. Nitrogen saturation in northern forest ecosystems-hypotheses and implications. BioScience. 39: 378–386.

Baron, J.S.; Rueth, H.M.; Wolfe, A.M. [and others]. 2000. Ecosystem responses to nitrogen deposition in the Colorado Front Range. Ecosystems. 3: 352–368.

Bruteig, I.E. 1993. The epiphytic lichen *Hypogymnia physodes* as a biomonitor of atmospheric nitrogen and sulphur deposition in Norway. Environmental Monitoring and Assessment. 26: 27–47.

Bytnerowicz, A.; Fenn, M. 1996. Nitrogen deposition in California forests: a review. Environmental Pollution. 92: 127–146.

Dufrêne, M.; Legendre, P. 1997. Species assemblages and indicator species: the need for a flexible asymmetrical approach. Ecological Monographs. 67: 345–366.

Eilers, J.M.; Rose, C.L.; Sullivan, T.J. 1994. Status of air quality and effects of atmospheric pollutants on ecosystems in the Pacific Northwest region of the National Park Service. Tech. Rep. NPS/NRAQD/NRTR–94/160. http://www2.nature.nps.gov/air/Pubs/pdf/reviews/pnw/PNWfinalreport1.pdf. [Date accessed: September 7, 2006].

Fenn, M.E.; Baron, J.S.; Allen, E.B. [and others]. 2003a. Ecological effects of nitrogen deposition in the Western United States. BioScience. 53: 404–420.

Fenn, M.E.; Haeuber, R.; Tonnesen, G.S. [and others]. 2003b. Nitrogen emissions, deposition, and monitoring in the Western United States. BioScience. 53: 391–403.

Fenn, M.E.; Poth, M.A.; Johnson, D.W. 1996. Evidence for nitrogen saturation in the San Bernadino Mountains in southern California. Forest Ecology and Management. 82: 211–230.

Gauslaa, Y. 1995. Lobarion, an epiphytic community of ancient forests, threatened by acid rain. Lichenologist. 27: 59–76.

Geiser, L. 2004. Manual for monitoring air quality using lichens on national forests of the Pacific Northwest. Tech. Pap. R6–NR–AQ–TP–1–04. Portland, OR: U.S. Department of Agriculture Forest Service, Pacific Northwest Region. 126 p.

Geiser, L.H.; Neitlich, P.N. 2007. Air pollution and climate gradients in western Oregon and Washington indicated by epiphytic macrolichens. Environmental Pollution. 145: 203–218.

Hawksworth, D.L.; Rose, F. 1970. Quantitative scale for estimating sulfur dioxide air pollution in England and Wales using epiphytic lichens. Nature (London). 227: 145–148.

Jovan, S.; McCune, B. 2005. Air-quality bioindication in the greater central valley of California, with epiphytic macrolichen communities. Ecological Applications. 15: 1712–1726.

Jovan, S.; McCune, B. 2006. Using epiphytic macrolichen communities for biomonitoring ammonia in forests of the greater Sierra Nevada, California. Water, Air, and Soil Pollution. 170: 69–93.

Kruskal, J.B. 1964. Non-metric multidimensional scaling: a numerical method. Psychometrika. 29: 115–129.

Lambley, P.; Wolseley, P., eds. 2004. Lichens in a changing pollution environment: papers presented at a workshop in Nettlecombe, Somerset. English Nat. Res. Rep. 525. Peterborough, UK: English Nature. 121 p. http://www.english-nature.org.uk/pubs/publication/PDF/525.pdf. [Date accessed: July 18, 2006].

Max, T.A.; Schreuder, H.T.; Hazard, J.W. [and others]. 1996. The Pacific Northwest region vegetation inventory and monitoring system. Res. Pap. PNW–RP–493. Portland, OR: U.S. Department of Agriculture Forest Service, Pacific Northwest Research Station. 22 p.

McCune, B. 1988. Lichen communities along O_3 and SO_2 gradients in Indianapolis. The Bryologist. 91: 223–228.

McCune, B.; Dey, J.P.; Peck, J.E. [and others]. 1997. Repeatability of community data: species richness versus gradient scores in large-scale lichen studies. The Bryologist. 100: 40–46.

McCune, B.; Grace, J.B. 2002. Analysis of ecological communities. Gleneden Beach, OR: MjM Software. 300 p.

McNab, W.H.; Avers, P.E., comps. 1994. Ecological subregions of the United States: section descriptions. WO–WSA–5. Washington, DC: U.S. Department of Agriculture Forest Service. 267 p.

Nash, T.H., III; Sigal, L.L. 1999. Epiphytic lichens in the San Bernardino Mountains in relation to oxidant gradients. In: Miller, P.R.; McBride, J.R., eds. Oxidant air pollutant impacts on the montane forests of southern California: a case study of the San Bernardino Mountains. Ecol. Studies 134. New York: Springer-Verlag: 223–234.

Oregon Department of Environmental Quality, Air Quality Division. 2005. 2004 Oregon air quality data summaries. Portland, OR. 91 p. http://www.deq.state.or.us/aq/forms/2004ar/2004ar-full.pdf. [Date accessed: July 18, 2006].

Porter, E.; Blett, T.; Potter, D.U.; Huber, C. 2005. Protecting resources on Federal lands: implications of critical loads for atmospheric deposition of nitrogen and sulfur. Bioscience. 55: 603–612.

Ruoss, E.; Vonarburg, C. 1995. Lichen diversity and ozone impact in rural areas of Central Switzerland. Cryptogamic Botany. 5: 252–263.

Søchting, U. 1995. Lichens as monitors of nitrogen deposition. Cryptogamic Botany. 5: 264–269.

U.S. Department of Agriculture Forest Service. 2006. Field instructions for the annual inventory of Washington, Oregon, California, and Alaska: supplement for phase 3 (FHM) indicators. Portland, OR: U.S. Department of Agriculture Forest Service, Pacific Northwest Research Station. 136 p. http://www.srs.fs.usda.gov/working/author/authors_guide-screen.pdf. [Date accessed: July 18].

Van Herk, C.M. 1999. Mapping of ammonia pollution with epiphytic lichens in the Netherlands. Lichenologist. 31: 9–20.

Introduction

Insects and diseases are a natural part of forested ecosystems. Their activity is partially regulated by biotic factors, e.g., host abundance, host quality; physical factors, e.g., soil, climate; and disturbances (Berryman 1986). Insects and diseases can influence both forest patterns and forest processes by causing, for example, defoliation and mortality. These effects may occur at small scales (gap phase) or large scales (forest development) and at any seral stage (Castello and others 1995). It can be useful to examine population trends for individual insect or pathogen species. However, for broadscale analysis, examining the cumulative effects of insects and pathogens gives a representation of ecosystem stress over time.

Methods

I used the nationally compiled Forest Service Forest Health Protection (FHP) aerial survey data from 1998 through 2004 (see footnote 3 in chapter 1) to assess insect and disease activity at the landscape level. The exposure of forests to mortality- and defoliation-causing agents was assessed within each Forest Health Monitoring (FHM) region. Exposure was defined as the area in hectares with mortality- or defoliation-causing agents present. The analysis was based on relative exposure (observed vs. expected) on a county basis within each FHM region and was used to identify currently active hotspots of activity (Coulston and Riitters 2003, Kulldorff 1997). Relative exposure could range from zero to infinity, where <1 represented low relative exposure and less-than-expected defoliation or mortality within the region. A value >1 represented more-than-expected exposure to defoliation- or mortality-causing agents within the FHM region of interest. The measure is linear, so, for example, a relative exposure value of 2 would indicate that an area had experienced twice the exposure expected for the region. While information from 1998 through 2004 was used to calculate the relative exposure, only counties with activity in 2004 have a relative exposure value greater than zero displayed on the maps.

Mortality-Causing Agents

In the Northeast FHM region, forest areas in ecoregion sections 211C—Fundy Coastal and Interior and 211B—Maine—New Brunswick Foothills and Lowlands experienced more than six times the expected exposure to mortality-causing agents from 1998–2004 (fig. 6.1). Balsam woolly adelgid accounted for most of this activity, which peaked in 2002; however, there was still activity in 2004. In the South FHM region, forested areas in sections 221J—Central Ridge and Valley, 221H—Northern Cumberland Plateau, M221D—Blue Ridge Mountains, and 231A—Southern Appalachian

Chapter 6. Insects and Diseases

JOHN W. COULSTON

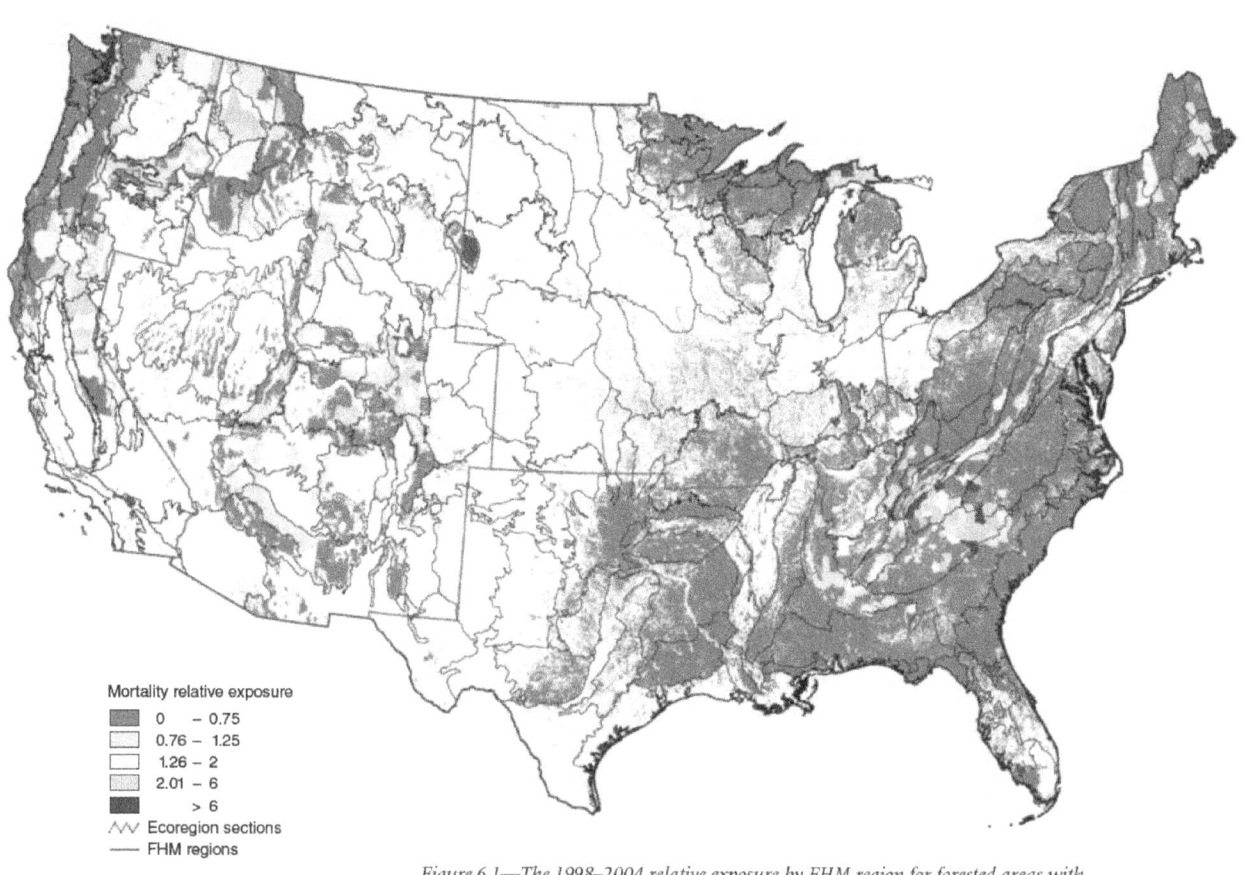

Mortality relative exposure

▨	0 – 0.75
☐	0.76 – 1.25
☐	1.26 – 2
▨	2.01 – 6
■	> 6
∧∧	Ecoregion sections
—	FHM regions

Figure 6.1—The 1998–2004 relative exposure by FHM region for forested areas with currently (2004) active mortality-causing agents. The gray lines delineate ecoregion sections (Cleland and others 2005, McNab and others 2005). Forest cover source was the U.S. Department of Agriculture Forest Service, Remote Sensing Applications Center. (Data source: U.S. Department of Agriculture Forest Service, Forest Health Protection)

Piedmont experienced more than six times the expected exposure to mortality-causing agents. This activity was attributable to southern pine beetle. Much of the forested area in section 221J—Central Ridge and Valley had a relative exposure of greater than six (fig. 6.1); however, the southern pine beetle activity in that section peaked in 2001 and has decreased since 2003 (fig. 6.2). In the North Central FHM region,

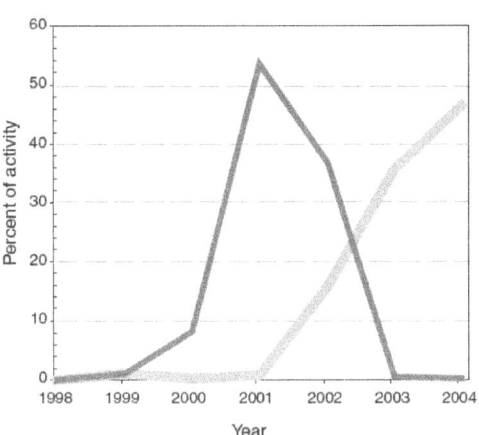

Central Ridge and Valley (221J)   Belt Mountains (M332D)

Figure 6.2—Temporal distribution of mortality-causing activity in ecoregion section 221J - Central Ridge and Valley. Most of the activity was attributable to southern pine beetle. Temporal distribution of defoliation-causing activity in ecoregion section M332D - Belt Mountains. Most of the activity was attributable to western spruce budworm. (Data Source: U.S. Department of Agriculture Forest Service, Forest Health Protection)

forested areas in sections M334A—Black Hills and 212R—Eastern Upper Peninsula had relative exposures of more than six (fig. 6.1). In section M334A—Black Hills, mountain pine beetle accounted for most of the activity. In section 212R—Eastern Upper Peninsula, beech bark disease caused most of the recorded mortality in 2004. In the Interior West FHM region, section M331I—Northern Parks and Ranges had some forested areas exposed to more than six times the expected activity. Most of the activity was attributable to mountain pine beetle, Douglas-fir beetle, fir engraver, and spruce beetle. In the West Coast FHM region, forested areas in section M262B—Southern California Mountain and Valley had more than six times the expected exposure rate to mortality-causing agents (fig. 6.1). Most of the mortality was attributed to bark beetles.

Defoliation-Causing Agents

Ecoregion section 221A—Lower New England in the Northeast FHM region had several areas exposed to more than six times the expected rate of defoliation-causing agents (fig. 6.3). In 2004, winter moth, forest tent caterpillar, and gypsy moth were active in this section. In the South FHM region, forest tent caterpillar continued to

49

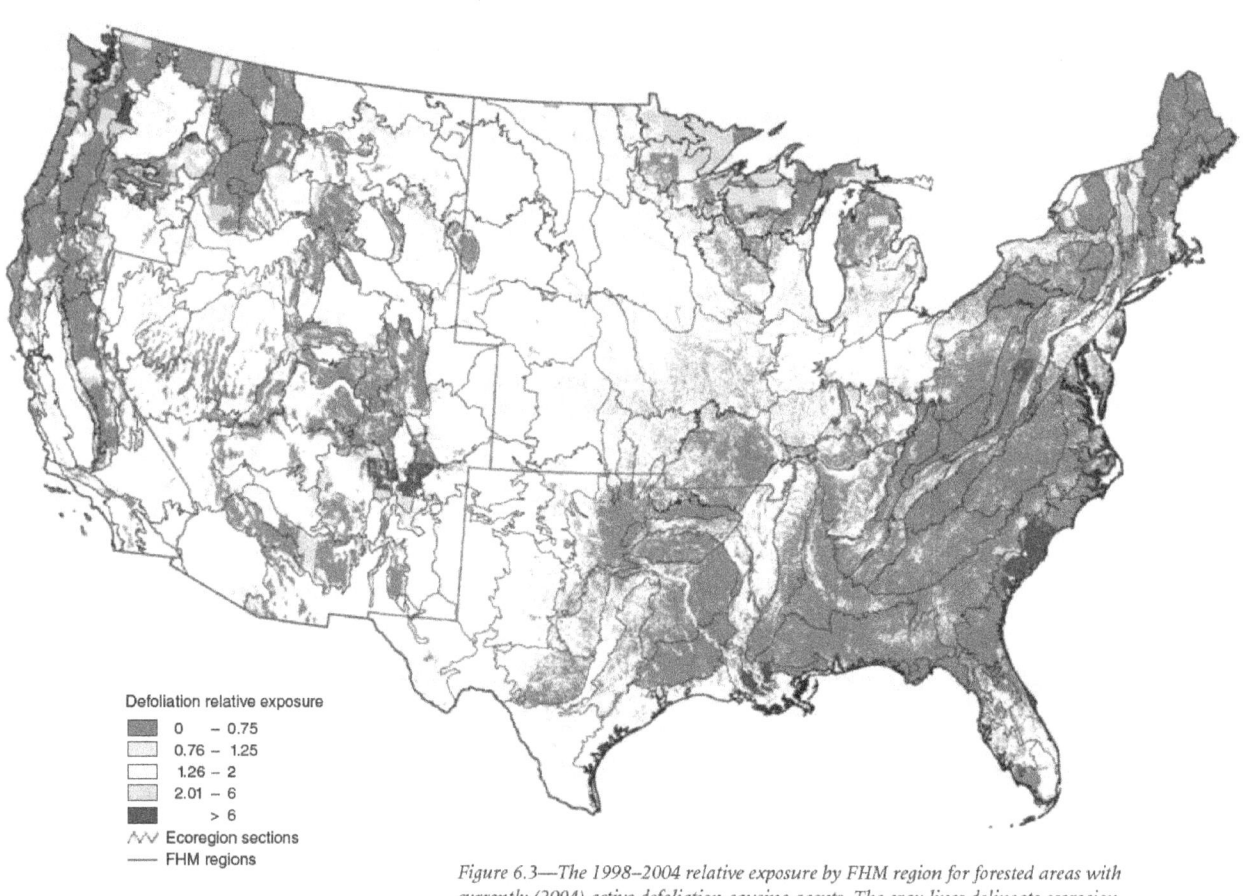

Defoliation relative exposure

    0   – 0.75
    0.76 – 1.25
    1.26 – 2
    2.01 – 6
       > 6
/\/\ Ecoregion sections
—— FHM regions

Figure 6.3—The 1998–2004 relative exposure by FHM region for forested areas with currently (2004) active defoliation-causing agents. The gray lines delineate ecoregion sections (Cleland and others 2005, McNab and others 2005). Forest cover source was the U.S. Department of Agriculture Forest Service, Remote Sensing Applications Center. (Data Source: U.S. Department of Agriculture Forest Service, Forest Health Protection)

defoliate parts of section 232C—Atlantic Coastal Flatwoods. In sections 232E—Louisiana Coastal Prairie and Marshes and 234C—Atchafalaya and Red River Alluvial Plains, bald cypress leaf roller and forest tent caterpillar contributed to defoliation in excess of six times the expected rate. In the North Central FHM region, forests in province 212—Laurentian Mixed Forest had relative exposures to defoliation-causing agents 2 to 5.99 times the expected rate (fig. 6.3). Several insects caused this defoliation including the spruce budworm, jack pine budworm, and eastern larch beetle. In the Interior West FHM region, sections M331F—Southern Parks and Rocky Mountain Range and M331G—South-Central Highlands had forested areas exposed to more than six times the expected exposure rate to defoliation-causing agents (fig. 6.3). Forests in section M332D—Belt Mountains in Montana also experienced more than six times the expected exposure to defoliation-causing agents (fig. 6.3). Most of the defoliation was caused by western spruce budworm activity, which has increased since 2001 (fig. 6.2). In the West Coast FHM region, forests in the northern part of section M242C—Eastern Cascades experienced more than six times the expected exposure rates (fig. 6.3).

Literature Cited

Berryman, A.A. 1986. Forest insects: principles and practice of population management. New York: Plenum Press. 279 p.

Castello, J.D.; Leopold, D.J.; Smallidge, P.J. 1995. Pathogens, patterns, and processes in forest ecosystems. BioScience. 45(1): 16–24.

Cleland, D.T.; Freeouf, J.A.; Keys, J.E. [and others]. 2005. Ecological subregions: sections and subsections for the conterminous United States. Washington, DC: U.S. Department of Agriculture Forest Service. [Map, presentation scale 1:3,500,000; colored]. [Also on CD–ROM as a Geographic Information System coverage in ArcINFO format].

Coulston, J.W.; Riitters, K.H. 2003. Geographic analysis of forest health indicators using spatial scan statistics. Environmental Management. 31: 764–773.

Kulldorff, M. 1997. A spatial scan statistic. Communications in Statistics: Theory and Methods. 26: 1481–1496.

McNab, W.H.; Cleland, D.T.; Freeouf, J.A. [and others], comps. 2005. Description of ecological subregions: sections of the conterminous United States [CD–ROM]. Washington, DC: U.S. Department of Agriculture Forest Service. 80 p.

Why Is Marine Cargo Important to Forest Health?

A major pathway for the introduction of nonindigenous forest pests is accidental transport on cargo imported from overseas. Diseases may be brought into the United States via commercial trade of nursery stock or other live plant material, as has been suggested for *Phytophthora ramorum*, the pathogen that causes sudden oak death (Ivors and others 2006). Insects may similarly hitchhike on live plants, but may be more commonly transported on or in raw logs, wood products, dunnage (materials used to space or brace cargo loads), and solid wood packing materials. Pallets, crates, and other materials used to protect and contain goods for shipment are often made from poor-quality wood that is in many cases not fully debarked (Campbell 2001). Such materials are particularly good vectors for bark beetles and wood boring insects, which can survive in the materials throughout the shipment duration (Brockerhoff and others 2006, Haack 2006).

With expanding global trade, the impacts of introduced pests on U.S. forests are likely to rise substantially (Levine and D'Antonio 2003).

Not all introduced species become established, but varieties that are well adapted to become established in U.S. forests are more likely to arrive if introductions of individual species increase (Campbell 2001). Currently, national-scale risk assessments quantify the level of threat that individual pests represent to the United States based on biological and other information gathered from other countries. Analyses of pest interception databases such as the U.S. Department of Agriculture, Animal and Plant Health Inspection Service (APHIS), Port Information Network (PIN) identify the pests most commonly detected during inspections at marine ports (e.g., Haack 2001, 2006; McCullough and others 2006), although only a small fraction (approximately 2 percent) of incoming cargo is subject to such inspection (National Research Council 2002). These analyses do not provide spatial information about which parts of the United States face the greatest risk from forest pest introductions. However, by analyzing statistical data on foreign cargo imports, it is possible to examine trends in the amount of high-risk cargo arriving at ports of entry as well as the geographic relationship of those ports to forested landscapes of the United

Chapter 7. Marine Cargo Imports and Forest Pest Introductions

Frank K. Koch

States. Such work yields a basic picture of where the risks from introduced forest pests are the greatest and may suggest locations in which to prioritize monitoring or management measures.

Methods

Data on foreign marine cargo imports were acquired from the U.S. Army Corps of Engineers Navigation Data Center (2006). The available data, spanning the years 1997 to 2004, were compiled into a table of more than 40,000 unique records. Each record lists the foreign port of origin, the U.S. marine port destination, and the weight tonnage (short tons) of a given commodity category unloaded at that port. Commodity categories are described by a two-digit code from the Navigation Data Center's Lock Performance Monitoring System (table 7.1).

The data coding system does not include a distinct category for live plants—the most likely pathway for forest pathogen introductions—so analysis was restricted to commodities on which forest insects are likely to be introduced. High-risk commodity categories were identified

Table 7.1—Commodity categories for U.S. marine cargo statistics data

Commodity code	Commodity description	Included in analysis
0	Units (ferried autos, passengers, railway cars)	
10	Coal, lignite, and coal coke	
20	Petroleum and petroleum products	
21	Crude petroleum	
22	Gasoline, jet fuel, kerosene	
23	Distillate, residual, and other fuel oils; lube oil and greases	
24	Petroleum pitches, coke, asphalt, naptha, and solvents	
29	Petroleum products not elsewhere classified	
30	Chemicals and related products	
31	Fertilizers	
32	Other chemicals and related products	
40	Crude materials, inedible except fuels	
41	Forest products, lumber, logs, woodchips	Yes
42	Pulp and waste paper	
43	Sand, gravel, stone, rock, limestone, soil, dredged material	Yes
44	Iron ore, iron and steel waste and scrap	
45	Marine shells	
46	Nonferrous ores and scrap	
47	Sulphur (dry), clay, and salt	
48	Slag	
49	Other nonmetallic minerals	
50	Primary manufactured goods	Yes
51	Paper and allied products	Yes
52	Building cement and concrete; lime; glass	Yes
53	Primary iron and steel products (ingots, bars, rods, etc.)	Yes
54	Primary nonferrous metal products; fabricated metal products	Yes

continued

Table 7.1—Commodity categories for U.S. marine cargo statistics data (continued)

Commodity code	Commodity description	Included in analysis
55	Primary wood products; veneer; plywood	Yes
60	Food and farm products	
61	Fish	
62	Wheat	
63	Corn	
64	Barley, rye, oats, rice, and sorghum grains	
65	Oilseeds (soybean, flaxseed, and others)	
66	Vegetable products	
67	Animal feed, grain mill products, flour, processed grains	
68	Other agricultural products; food and kindred products	
70	All manufactured equipment, machinery and products	Yes
80	Waste material; garbage, landfill, sewage sludge, waste water	
89	Waste and scrap not elsewhere classified	
90 or 99	Unknown or not elsewhere classified	

based on the types of cargo associated with forest insects in the APHIS PIN database: forest products or commodities that are typically shipped with wood packaging (table 7.1). Two-digit commodity codes offer limited thematic resolution, so some of the identified categories include goods that are regularly wood packaged and others that typically do not involve wood packing materials. These categories were used in the analysis under the assumption that a substantial proportion of their total tonnage involved some wood packaging, and that proportions did not vary much between ports, and so would not affect the ports' relative rankings in terms of total imports.

The total tonnage of all selected commodities arriving between 1997 and 2004 was calculated for each of the ports, which were then mapped based on coordinates from the U.S. National Transportation Atlas Databases (U.S. Department of Transportation, Bureau of Transportation Statistics 2005). To illustrate possible geographic relationships between ports and introduced pests, county-level distributions of several forest insects that have emerged in the United States during the last 10 years (table 7.2) were mapped in combination with the ports. The selected insect pests have already caused mortality in U.S. forest species or represent a high risk of establishment and spread.

Some marine cargo is shipped in large metal containers that are not opened prior to reaching their final inland destination. Nevertheless, a substantial majority (95 percent CI = 64 ± 1 percent) of freight tonnage is shipped 160 km

(100 miles) or less within the United States, regardless of transport mode (U.S. Department of Transportation, Bureau of Transportation Statistics; U.S. Department of Commerce, U.S. Census Bureau 2005). Furthermore, marine port terminals and their nearby distribution facilities receive a large quantity of crating, dunnage, and other materials that may harbor forest pests. These packing materials may sit in open air for some time (Campbell 2001), and a flying insect might move from these materials to forested

Table 7.2—Notable forest insect pests detected in the United States since 1996

Species	First detected	Description
Asian longhorned beetle (*Anoplophora glabripennis*)	1996	Causes mortality in a variety of hardwood species. Infestations have already caused damage in a few U.S. urban areas, leading to extensive quarantine and eradication efforts (U.S. Department of Agriculture, APHIS 2006).
Redbay ambrosia beetle (*Xyleborus glabratus*)	2002	Pest of Lauraceae family. In the United States, has been associated with mortality of redbay (*Persea borbonia*) and has been detected on sassafras (*Sassafras albidum*). Uncertain if it will have a major economic impact (Haack 2006, Rabaglia 2003).
Emerald ash borer (*Agrilus plannipennis*)	2002	Causes significant mortality of ash (*Fraxinus*) species. Has spread beyond quarantine zones in both the United States and Canada (McCullough and Katovich 2004).
Sirex wood wasp (*Sirex noctilio*)	2004	Major pest of *Pinus* plantations in New Zealand, Australia, South Africa, and South America. Usually attacks stressed trees first (Hoebeke and others 2005).
Mediterranean pine engraver *Orthotomicus erosus*)	2004	Pest of many *Pinus* species in the Mediterranean, Middle East, Central Asia, and China with numerous suitable hosts throughout the United States. Usually does not attack healthy trees (Lee and others 2005).

areas within its flight range, which could be tens of kilometers for a strong flier or under favorable weather conditions (Dingle 1972, Pedgley 1993). To highlight the elevated risk of introduction in forested areas proximal to ports, U.S. ecoregion sections (Cleland and others 2005) were ranked according to the percentage of their total forested area that fell within a 160-km (100-mile) buffer around one of the ports identified by tonnage analysis. Susceptible forest areas were determined by intersecting the buffer with a forest distribution map developed from Moderate Resolution Imaging Spectoradiometer (MODIS) satellite imagery (250 m spatial resolution).

What Do the Data Show?

Between 1997 and 2004, 171 ports in the conterminous United States (fig. 7.1) received some tonnage of high-risk commodities. Two neighboring California ports (Los Angeles and Long Beach) had the highest total tonnages by a large margin, together receiving more than 270 million tons (table 7.3). When combined, the two biggest ports in the State of Washington (Seattle and Tacoma) received more than 82 million tons, somewhat less than the amount received at the port area of New York City[1]

(approximately 89 million tons). Three ports clustered on the Southeastern United States coast—Charleston, SC; Savannah, GA; and Jacksonville, FL—ranked among the top 15 ports in the country. The Gulf of Mexico has several closely spaced ports, including several in the vicinity of the major ports of Houston, TX, and New Orleans, LA. No ports of the Great Lakes region ranked among the highest in tonnage, but the region has numerous, closely spaced ports that accepted low-to-moderate tonnages between 1997 and 2004.

For the five example insects (fig. 7.1), there appears to be strong correspondence between insect spatial distribution and marine port proximity. Only the distribution of the Mediterranean pine engraver does not directly overlap a major U.S. marine port or adjacent urban area. While this pest may have been introduced to the area by a different pathway, e.g., air cargo, several major marine ports are nearby, especially in the Los Angeles area, and the pest has commonly been intercepted from solid wood packing materials at U.S. marine ports (Lee and others 2005). Notably, these pests are emblematic of other recent invaders; for example, the Mediterranean pine engraver is

---

[1] Tonnage for New York City actually includes the total tonnage for port facilities in the New York City boroughs as well as ports across the Hudson River in New Jersey.

High-risk imports, 1997–2004
total tonnage (millions)

- ○   < 5
- ●   5 – 10
- ●   10 – 25
- ●   25 – 50
- ●   > 50

▨ Asian longhorned beetle
▨ Redbay ambrosia beetle
▨ Emerald ash borer
▨ Sirex woodwasp
▨ Mediterranean pine engraver
— State boundary

Figure 7.1—United States marine ports of entry ranked by tonnage of high-risk imports, combined with the spatial distribution of five forest insect pests. (County-level insect spatial data sources: asian longhorned beetle, http://ceris.purdue.edu/napis/maps/pstsurvey.html; redbay ambrosia beetle, Florida Department of Agriculture and Consumer Services, Forestry Division, and the Georgia Forestry Commission; emerald ash borer, http://eabviewer.rsgis.msu.edu/viewer.htm; sirex woodwasp, New York State Department of Agriculture and Markets, Division of Plant Industry; Mediterranean pine engraver, U.S. Department of Agriculture Forest Service. Forest cover source was the U.S. Department of Agriculture Forest Service, Remote Sensing Applications Center. Additional data source: U.S. Department of Transportation, Bureau of Transportation Statistics)

Table 7.3—Top 15 U.S. ports in terms of total tonnage of high-risk imports (1997–2004)[a]

Port	Tonnage
	short tons
Long Beach, CA	137,358,748
Los Angeles, CA	133,026,491
Houston, TX	90,569,953
New York, NY, and NJ	89,073,733
New Orleans, LA	70,462,491
Seattle, WA	55,151,673
Charleston, SC	48,358,707
Baltimore, MD	44,666,152
Savannah, GA	38,998,758
Port of South Louisiana, LA	35,981,554
Norfolk Harbor, VA	32,282,798
Jacksonville, FL	28,455,220
Tacoma, WA	26,988,061
Tampa, FL	25,160,558
Philadelphia, PA	23,691,829

[a]High-risk commodity categories were identified based on the types of cargo associated with forest insects in the U.S. Department of Agriculture, Animal and Plant Health Inspection Service, Port Information Network database: forest products or commodities that are typically shipped with wood packaging (table 7.1).

one of four new bark beetle species believed to have been established in the United States since 2000 (Haack 2006).

Certain regions are of particular concern because of the large proportion of potentially susceptible forest within a short distance of high-tonnage marine ports. Of the 190 ecoregion sections in the conterminous United States, 37 had more than 95 percent of their forested area within 160 km (100 miles) of a marine port of entry (fig. 7.2). On the Pacific Coast, these included a heavily forested section, M242A—Oregon and Washington Coast Ranges, as well as two sparsely forested sections, 261B—Southern California Coast and M262B—Southern California Mountain and Valley. All of the ecoregion sections surrounding Lake Michigan fell mostly within the buffer zone. These sections include three heavily forested ones: 212S—Northern Upper Peninsula, 212R—Eastern Upper Peninsula, and 212H—Northern Lower Peninsula. In New England, most ecoregion sections had more than 60 percent of their forested area with 100 miles of a high-risk port. In the Southeast, the heavily forested 232C—Atlantic Coastal Flatwoods section may face

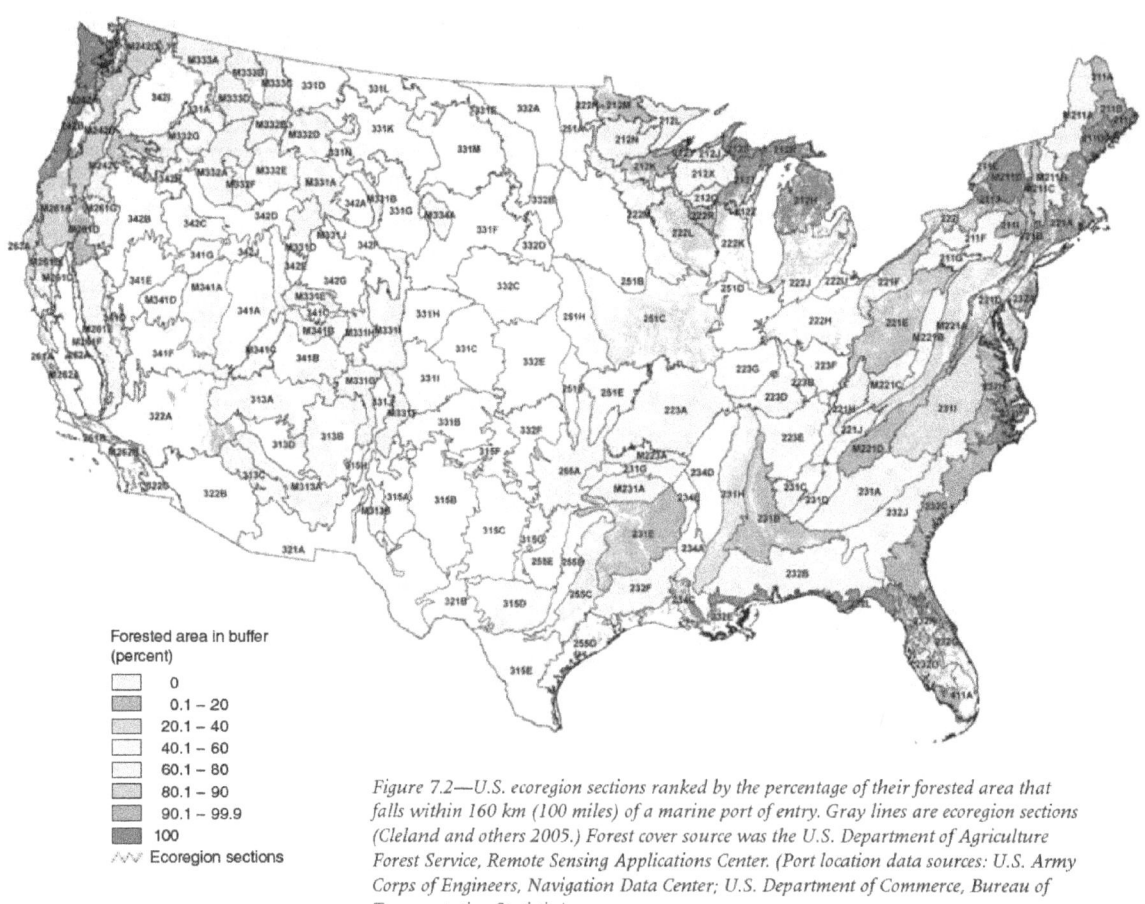

Figure 7.2—U.S. ecoregion sections ranked by the percentage of their forested area that falls within 160 km (100 miles) of a marine port of entry. Gray lines are ecoregion sections (Cleland and others 2005.) Forest cover source was the U.S. Department of Agriculture Forest Service, Remote Sensing Applications Center. (Port location data sources: U.S. Army Corps of Engineers, Navigation Data Center; U.S. Department of Commerce, Bureau of Transportation Statistics)

Forested area in buffer
(percent)

0
0.1 – 20
20.1 – 40
40.1 – 60
60.1 – 80
80.1 – 90
90.1 – 99.9
100
/\/\/ Ecoregion sections

particularly severe risk, with the combination of three major ports (Charleston, Savannah, and Jacksonville), several minor ports, and climatic conditions that are suitable for insect pest persistence. Another section, 232L—Gulf Coastal Lowlands, may face a similar threat level.

As noted, several assumptions about what should be considered high risk must be made when using these data. For example, the limited thematic resolution of the data, i.e., a lack of specific categories for nursery stock or other live plant material, did not permit assessment of forest pathogen introduction risk as distinct from insect pest risk. More generally, the marine port data presented here are only a part of the total forest pest risk from international trade. Similar datasets are available for land border crossings, airports, and ports along inland waterways of the United States, so a fuller examination would reconcile these datasets with the marine cargo data to create a more comprehensive national picture. It is also important to note that this analysis did not address the role of domestic transport of commodities after they are received at U.S. marine ports. While it may appear that the greatest risk of forest pest introductions is

associated with areas relatively close to marine ports, individual cargo shipments may travel long distances. Indeed, although more than 55 percent of marine cargo tonnage imported into the United States in 2002 remained in the same statistical region as the port of entry, approximately 14 percent of the nation's freight tonnage in 2002, regardless of origin, traveled distances of 500 miles or more (U.S. Department of Transportation, Bureau of Transportation Statistics; U.S. Department of Commerce, U.S. Census Bureau 2005) (U.S. Department of Transportation, Federal Highway Administration, Office of Freight Management and Operations 2006). For example, the banded elm bark beetle, first detected in baited traps in Colorado and Utah in 2003 but since found extensively throughout the Intermountain West (fig. 7.3), may have been introduced via this kind of long-distance shipment (Lee and others 2006, Liu and Haack 2003). Essentially, since a single infested cargo shipment may potentially result in a specific pest's introduction, and given the nation's well-developed transportation infrastructure, virtually every forested location in the conterminous United States faces some risk from pests introduced by international trade.

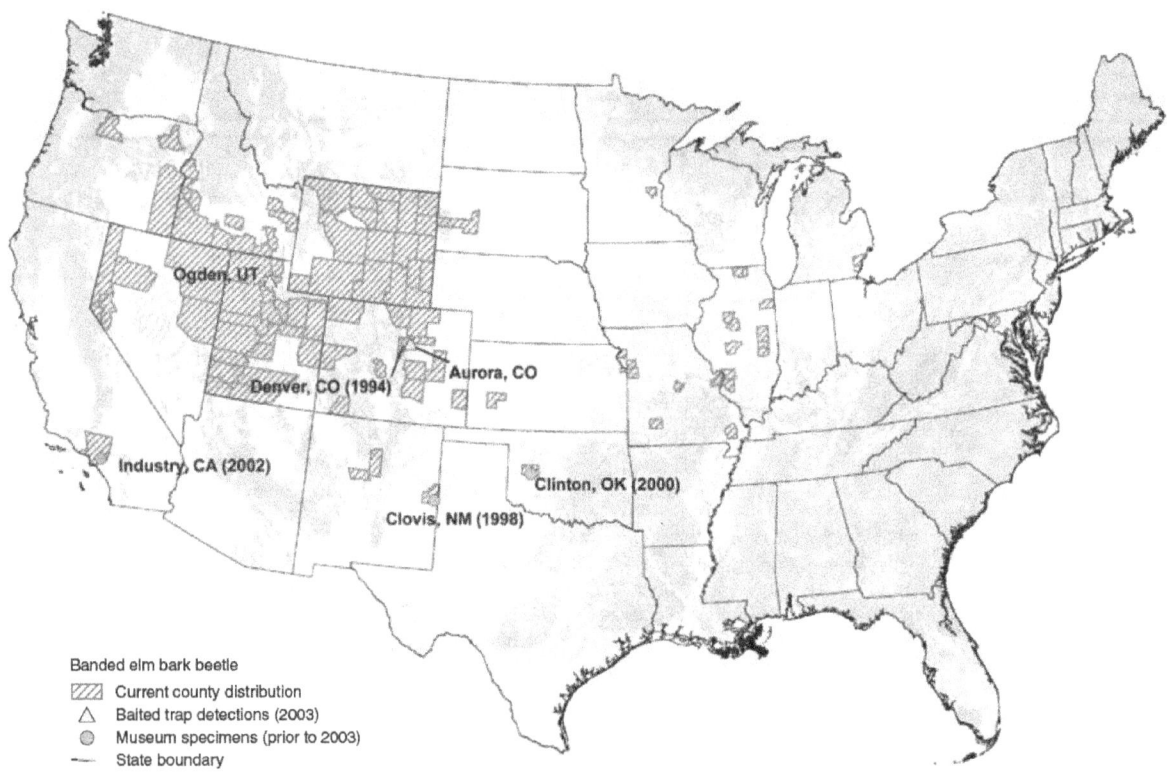

Banded elm bark beetle

▨ Current county distribution
△ Baited trap detections (2003)
◉ Museum specimens (prior to 2003)
— State boundary

Figure 7.3—Current county-level distribution of the banded elm bark beetle, Scolytus
schevyrewi. *Although first detected in baited traps in 2003, museum specimens suggest that
the pest was likely introduced to the Intermountain West region by the early 1990s. Forest cover
source was the U.S. Department of Agriculture Forest Service, Remote Sensing Applications Center.
[Distribution data source: U.S. Department of Agriculture Forest Service, Alien Forest Pest Explorer,
http://www.fs.fed.us/ne/morgantown/4557/AFPE/data.html. Locations of the first trap detections,
as well as museum specimens collected prior to 2003, were reported in Lee and others (2006)]*

Treatment of wood packaging materials could greatly reduce the risk of pest introductions. In 2004, the U.S. Department of Agriculture issued a rule requiring heat treatment or fumigation of wood packaging materials for cargo imported into the United States, but such practices have not yet been standardized worldwide, and will not eliminate all introduction risk (Haack 2006) [U.S. Department of Agriculture, Animal and Plant Health Inspection Service. 7 CFR Part 319 – importation of wood packaging materials. Federal Register 69(179): 55 719–55 733 (16 September 2004)]. In the meantime, increased monitoring in high-risk forested areas may catch pests before they become established problems, thus substantially reducing control costs. This is consistent with the observations of a recent U.S. Government Accountability Office (2006) report on forest pests, which advocates increased systematic monitoring of urban forests, particularly in port cities.

Literature Cited

Brockerhoff, E.G.; Bain, J.; Kimberley, M.; Knížek, M. 2006. Interception frequency of exotic bark and ambrosia beetles (Coleoptera: Scolytinae) and relationship with establishment in New Zealand and worldwide. Canadian Journal of Forest Research. 36: 289–298.

Campbell, F.T. 2001. The science of risk assessment for phytosanitary regulation and the impact of changing trade regulations. BioScience. 51(2): 148–153.

Cleland, D.T.; Freeouf, J.A.; Keys, J.E. [and others]. 2005. Ecological subregions: sections and subsections for the conterminous United States. Washington, DC: U.S. Department of Agriculture Forest Service. [Map, presentation scale 1:3,500,000; colored]. [Also available on CD–ROM consisting of Geographic Information System coverage in ArcINFO format].

Dingle, H. 1972. Migration strategies of insects. Science. 175(4028): 1327–1335.

Haack, R.A. 2001. Intercepted Scolytidae (Coleoptera) at U.S. ports of entry: 1985-2000. Integrated Pest Management Reviews. 6: 253–282.

Haack, R.A. 2006. Exotic bark- and wood-boring Coleoptera in the United States: recent establishments and interceptions. Canadian Journal of Forest Research. 36: 269–288.

Hoebeke, E.R.; Haugen, D.A.; Haack, R.A. 2005. *Sirex noctilio*: discovery of a palearctic siricid woodwasp in New York. Newsletter of the Michigan Entomological Society. 50(1–2): 24–25.

Ivors, K.; Garbelotto, M.; Vries, D.E. [and others]. 2006. Microsatellite markers identify three lineages of *Phytophthora ramorum* in U.S. nurseries, yet single lineages in U.S. forest and European nursery populations. Molecular Ecology. 15: 1493–1505.

Lee, J.C.; Négron, J.F.; McElwey, S.J. [and others]. 2006. Pest alert: banded elm bark beetle – *Scolytus schevyrewi*. R2–PR–01–06. Golden, CO: U.S. Department of Agriculture Forest Service, Rocky Mountain Region, Forest Health Protection. 2 p.

Lee, J.C.; Smith, S.L.; Seybold, S.J. 2005. Pest alert: Mediterranean pine engraver. R5–PR–016. Davis, CA: U.S. Department of Agriculture Forest Service, State and Private Forestry, Pacific Southwest Region. 4 p. http://www.fs.fed.us/r5/spf/publications/pestalerts/Med_pine_engraver.pdf. [Date accessed: July 20, 2006].

Levine, J.M.; D'Antonio, C.M. 2003. Forecasting biological invasions with increasing international trade. Conservation Biology. 17(1): 322–326.

Liu, H.; Haack, R.A. 2003. Pest report: *Scolytus schevyrewi*. Exotic Forest Pest Information System (EXFOR), North American Forest Commission. http://spfnic.fs.fed.us/exfor/data/pestreports.cfm?pestidval=163&langdisplay=english. [Date accessed: October 23, 2006].

McCullough, D.G.; Katovich, S.A. 2004. Pest alert: emerald ash borer. NA–PR–02–04. Newtown Square, PA: U.S. Department of Agriculture Forest Service, State and Private Forestry, Northeastern Area. 2 p. http://na.fs.fed.us/spfo/pubs/pest_al/eab/eab04.htm. [Date accessed: July 20, 2006].

McCullough, D.G.; Work, T.T.; Cavey, J.F. [and others]. 2006. Interceptions of nonindigenous plant pests at U.S. ports of entry and border crossings over a 17-year period. Biological Invasions. 8: 611–630.

National Research Council, Committee on the Scientific Basis for Predicting the Invasive Potential of Nonindigenous Plants and Plant Pests in the United States, Board on Agriculture and Natural Resources. 2002. Predicting invasions of nonindigenous plants and plant pests. Washington, DC: National Academy Press. 195 p.

Pedgley, D.E. 1993. Managing migratory insect pests—a review. International Journal of Pest Management. 39(1): 3–12.

Rabaglia, R. 2003. Pest report: *Xyleborus glabratus*. Exotic Forest Pest Information System (EXFOR), North American Forest Commission. http://spfnic.fs.fed.us/exfor/data/pestreports.cfm?pestidval=148&langdisplay=english. [Date accessed: May 19, 2006].

U.S. Army Corps of Engineers, Navigation Data Center. 2006. U.S. waterway data: foreign cargo (inbound and outbound) for 1997–2004. http://www.iwr.usace.army.mil/ndc/data/dataimex.htm. [Date accessed: October 23].

U.S. Department of Agriculture, Animal and Plant Health Inspection Service. 2006. Asian longhorned beetle. APHIS Plant Protection and Quarantine, Emergency and Domestic Programs. http://www.aphis.usda.gov/ppq/ep/alb/. [Date accessed: May 22].

U.S. Department of Transportation, Bureau of Transportation Statistics. 2005. NTAD 2005 (National Transportation Atlas Databases 2005) [CD–ROM]. Washington, DC.

U.S. Department of Transportation, Bureau of Transportation Statistics; U.S. Department of Commerce, U.S. Census Bureau. 2005. Commodity flow survey 2002. C1–E02–ECFS–00–US1 [CD–ROM]. Washington, DC.

U.S. Department of Transportation, Federal Highway Administration, Office of Freight Management and Operations. 2006. Freight analysis framework (FAF²) commodity-origin database 2002. http://www.ops.fhwa.dot.gov/freight/freight%5Fanalysis/faf/. [Date accessed: October 23].

U.S. Government Accountability Office. 2006. Invasive forest pests: lessons learned from three recent infestations may aid in managing future efforts. Report to the Chairman, Committee on Natural Resources, House of Representatives, April 2006. GAO–06–353. Washington, DC. 118 p.

Introduction

Photosynthetic capacity is dependent upon the size and condition of the tree crown. Trees with full, vigorous crowns are generally associated with more vigorous growth rates (Zarnoch and others 2004). Therefore, the Forest Service Forest Inventory and Analysis (FIA) Program measures a suite of crown condition indicators to evaluate forest health. Among the crown condition indicators are crown dieback and two measures of foliage abundance, crown density and foliage transparency. Crown density is the amount of crown biomass, i.e., branches, foliage, and reproductive structures, that blocks light visibility through the projected crown outline. Foliage transparency is the amount of skylight visible through the live, normally foliated portion of the crown, and crown dieback is the recent mortality of branches with fine twigs, which begins at the terminal portion of a branch and proceeds inward toward the trunk. All three variables are determined by means of ocular estimates to the nearest 5 percent.[1] High levels of crown dieback indicate potentially serious declines in tree health, while low levels of crown density and high levels of transparency may indicate greater amounts of defoliation and signal that a tree may have a reduced capacity for growth.

Analysis

There are various ways to examine the crown condition data for trends in forest health. For this report, the plot-level crown indicator values were mapped to reveal any spatial patterns of crown condition and identify areas having relatively high or low indicator values. Average crown conditions were calculated for softwood and hardwood species groups for each plot. Because crown condition averages at the hardwood or softwood level might mask important patterns at the species level, plot-level averages were calculated for smaller groupings of individual species as well. These smaller groupings generally followed the species groups established by FIA (appendix table A.1). Although all species groupings were examined, maps for only the most abundant species are presented.

Foliage transparency was originally developed as a measure of insect and disease defoliation of hardwoods for the North American Sugar Maple

KaDonna C. Randolph

---

[1] U.S. Department of Agriculture Forest Service. 2005. Forest inventory and analysis national core field guide, section 12 – crowns: measurements and sampling. Version 3.0. U.S. Department of Agriculture Forest Service, Washington Office. Internal report. On file with: U.S. Department of Agriculture Forest Service, Forest Inventory and Analysis, Rosslyn Plaza, 1620 North Kent Street, Arlington, VA 22209.

Decline Project, whereas crown density was developed as a measure of crown fullness and growth potential among loblolly and shortleaf pines in the Southern United States (Millers and others 1992). Both indicators were adapted by Forest Health Monitoring (FHM) and applied to all species; however, in this report crown density averages are reported only for softwood species and foliage transparency averages only for hardwood species. Average crown dieback is reported for all species groupings. A plot average was not included in the spatial evaluation if the plot contained fewer than five trees (diameter $\geq$5.0 inches) in a given species group. Available data from all FIA phase 3 plots collected between 2000 and 2004 were included in this analysis (table 8.1). Due to differences in data collection cycles and data processing timeframes among the FIA regions this resulted in an uneven distribution of plots across the country. Analyses were based on plots with perturbed ("fuzzed") geographic coordinates (McRoberts and others 2005).

Available thresholds defining the point at which trees begin to decline biologically (e.g., Steinman 2000) have not taken into account

Table 8.1—Years of data[a] included in the crown condition analysis by State

Years	States
2000–2004	IN, IA, MI, MN, MO, PA, UT, WI
2000–2003	ME
2000–2002, 2004	AL, AR, GA, KY, LA, NC, SC, TN, VA
2001–2004	AZ, CA, IL, KS, NE, OH, OR, SD
2001, 2003–2004	ND
2001–2002, 2004	FL, TX
2002–2004	CO, WA
2002–2003	NH, NY
2003–2004	CT, MA, MT, VT
2004	ID, MD, NE, NJ, RI, WV

[a]Data for the Southern States were obtained from U.S. Forest Service, Southern Research Station, FIA; all other data obtained from FIA Data Mart (http://www.ncrs2.fs.fed.us/FIADatamart/fiadatamart.aspx). [Date Accessed: April 2006].

species-specific differences in typical crown form. As a result, the risk of erroneously classifying trees as unhealthy may be high for some species. Therefore, plots are not classified as having healthy or unhealthy crowns in this report. Instead, spatial clusters of plots with high crown dieback, high foliage transparency, or low crown density averages relative to the other plots were identified visually by analyst interpretation as areas with potential forest health problems. The breakpoints in the figure legends were selected according to the distribution of plot averages for each indicator and in such a way as to best highlight the overall conclusions of the visual inspection.

What Do the Data Show?

Softwoods—Figures 8.1A and 8.1B show plot-level crown dieback and crown density averages across the conterminous United States for the softwood species group. Plot-level dieback averages were typically <10 percent with only a few scattered plots averaging more than 20 percent dieback. Plot-level crown density averages typically ranged between 36 and 55 percent. Spatial clusters of relatively high dieback were observed in Arizona, Utah, and Pennsylvania. Further examination of the species-specific plot averages in the West (fig. 8.2) indicated that the plots in Arizona and Utah consisted primarily of pinyon and juniper

species (see appendix table A.1). Plot-level dieback averages for this species group ranged between 0.0 and 32.7 percent; 7.6 percent of the plots had dieback averages >10 percent (fig. 8.2D). This clustering of relatively high dieback is likely evidence of the ongoing decline in the pinyon-juniper forest type, which has been caused by prolonged drought and insect and disease outbreaks (Shaw and others 2005). Pinyon pine mortality has been increasing since 2000, and in 2003 over 3.7 million acres were impacted throughout Arizona, California, Colorado, Nevada, New Mexico, and Utah (U.S. Department of Agriculture Forest Service 2005).

Examination of the cluster of plots with relatively high (>10 percent) crown dieback averages in Pennsylvania indicated a species mix of pine (*Pinus resinosa*, *P. rigida*, *P. strobus*, *P. sylvestris*, and *P. virginiana*) and eastern hemlock. Individual eastern hemlock and Scotch pine trees had the highest levels of crown dieback on these plots.

(A)

Percent crown dieback;
plot averages

o   0 – 9
◉   10 – 20
●   21 – 100

Figure 8.1—Crown dieback (A) and crown density (B) plot averages for softwood trees in the United States. Plot locations are approximate. (Data source: U.S. Department of Agriculture Forest Service, FIA Program) (continued to next page)

(B)

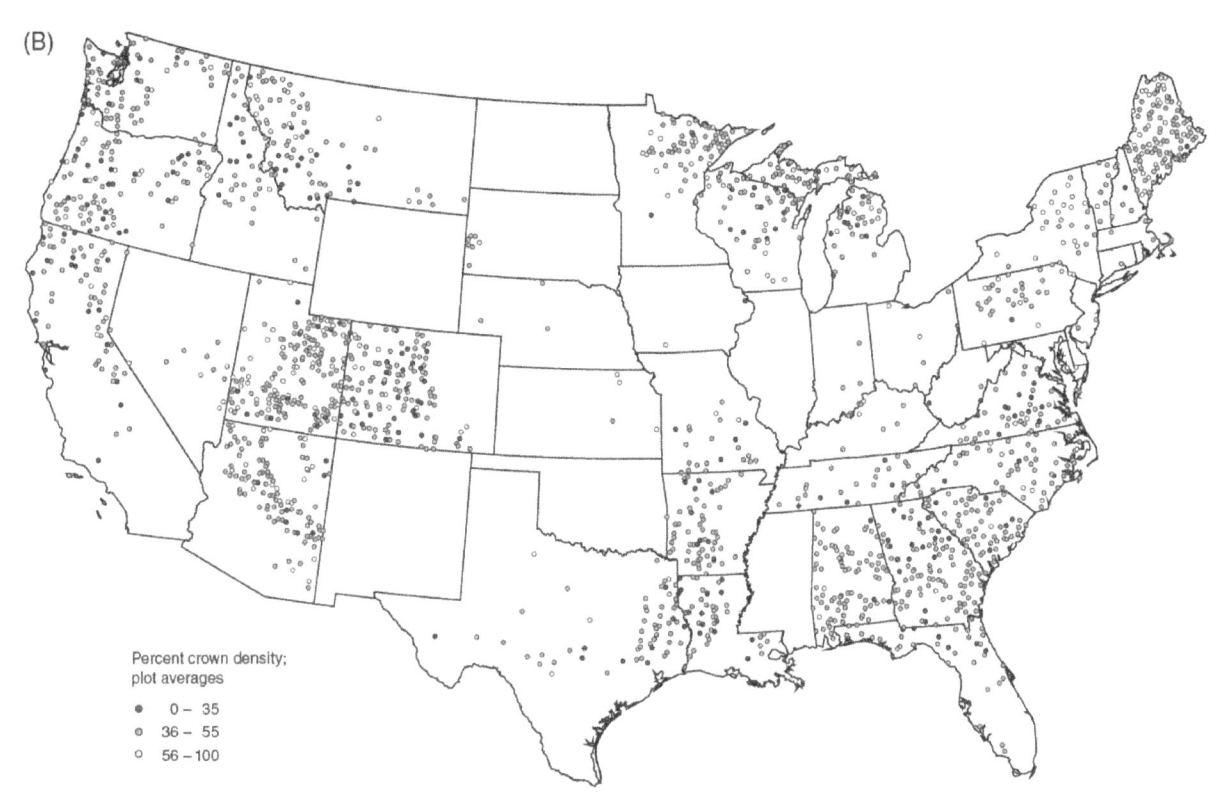

Percent crown density;
plot averages

- ● 0 – 35
- ◐ 36 – 55
- ○ 56 – 100

*Figure 8.1 (continued)—Crown dieback (A) and crown density
(B) plot averages for softwood trees in the United States. Plot
locations are approximate. (Data source: U.S. Department of
Agriculture Forest Service, FIA Program)*

(A)

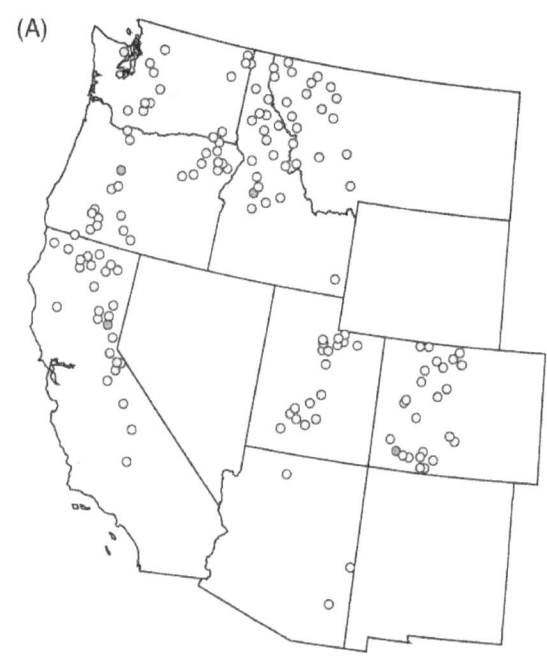

Percent crown dieback;
plot averages

○   0 – 9
◉   10 – 20
●   21 – 100

(B)

Percent crown dieback;
plot averages

○   0 – 9
◉   10 – 20
●   21 – 100

*Figure 8.2—Crown dieback plot averages for major softwood species
of the Western United States: (A) true fir, (B) Englemann spruce
and other spruces, (C) lodgepole pine, (D) pinyon pine and juniper,
(E) Douglas-fir, and (F) ponderosa and Jeffrey pine. Plot locations
are approximate. (Data source: U.S. Department of Agriculture
Forest Service, FIA Program) (continued to next page)*

(C)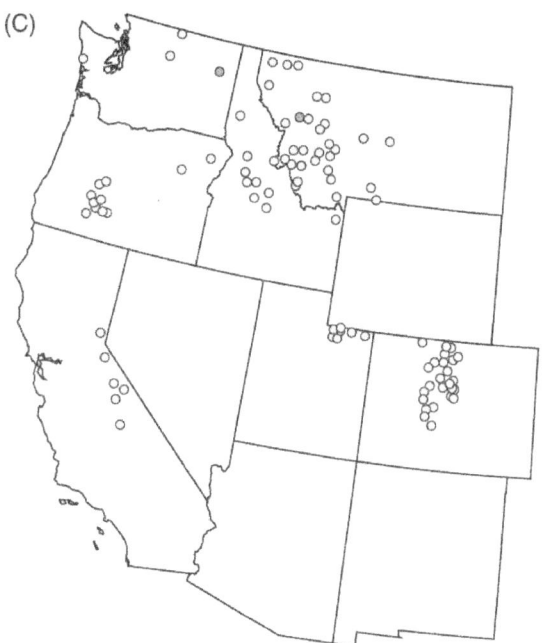

(D)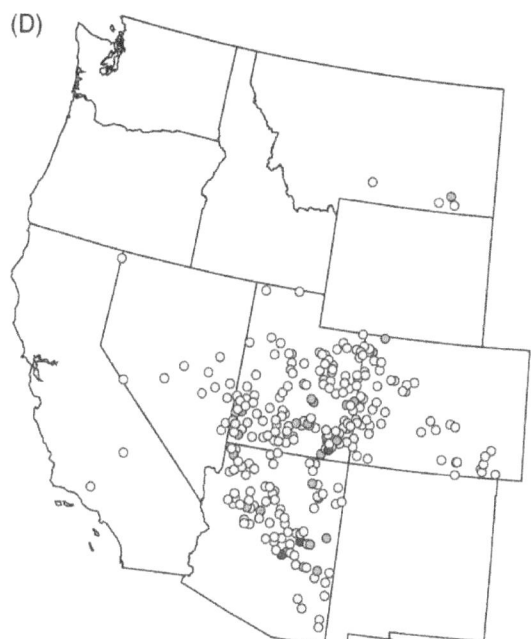

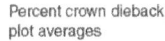
Percent crown dieback;
plot averages

○   0 – 9
◉   10 – 20
●   21 – 100

Percent crown dieback;
plot averages

○   0 – 9
◉   10 – 20
●   21 – 100

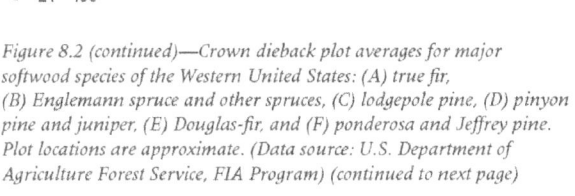
*Figure 8.2 (continued)—Crown dieback plot averages for major
softwood species of the Western United States: (A) true fir,
(B) Englemann spruce and other spruces, (C) lodgepole pine, (D) pinyon
pine and juniper, (E) Douglas-fir, and (F) ponderosa and Jeffrey pine.
Plot locations are approximate. (Data source: U.S. Department of
Agriculture Forest Service, FIA Program) (continued to next page)*

(E)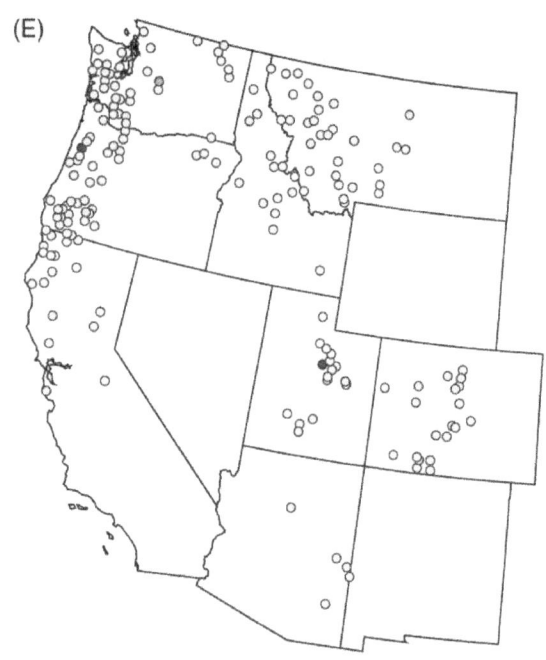

(F)

Percent crown dieback;
plot averages

○   0 –   9
◉   10 – 20
●   21 – 100

Percent crown dieback;
plot averages

○   0 –   9
◉   10 – 20
●   21 – 100

*Figure 8.2 (continued)—Crown dieback plot averages for major
softwood species of the Western United States: (A) true fir,
(B) Englemann spruce and other spruces, (C) lodgepole pine,
(D) pinyon pine and juniper, (E) Douglas-fir, and (F) ponderosa
and Jeffrey pine. Plot locations are approximate. (Data source:
U.S. Department of Agriculture Forest Service, FIA Program)*

Species-specific plot averages in the East (fig. 8.3) indicated that levels of crown dieback were relatively high for northern white-cedar, particularly in parts of Maine and Michigan. Plot averages for northern white-cedar ranged from 0.0 to 32.9 percent dieback; 16.0 percent of the plots had dieback averages >10 percent (fig. 8.3C. In an evaluation of forest health conditions between 1993 and 2002, Steinman (2004) mapped the percent of basal area with unhealthy crowns by county for several individual species in the Northeastern United States. Trees were said to have unhealthy crowns if any of the following conditions were met: at least 25 percent crown dieback, at least 30 percent foliage transparency, and <35 percent crown density. Clusters of plots with elevated dieback in northern white-cedar (fig. 8.3C) generally correspond to counties Steinman identified as having high percentages of northern white-cedar basal area with unhealthy crowns. Reasons why a relatively high proportion of plots have elevated levels of dieback are unclear although Johnston (1990) notes that unfavorable winter weather, deicing salts, and drought are common agents that may cause foliage discoloration and lead to severe damage or death of the tree. Maine experienced one of the worst droughts in its history between 1999 and 2002 (Lombard 2004), and dry conditions also occurred between 1998 and 2002 in the Upper Peninsula and northern Lower Peninsula of Michigan (Steinman 2004). Drought is a potential explanation, but further investigation is warranted.

Softwood crown density plot averages varied across the country (fig. 8.1B). The areas with the densest crowns corresponded to the pinyon-juniper and spruce-fir species groups in the West and East, respectively, whereas the areas with less dense crowns were dominated primarily by pine species (figs. 8.4A through 8.4F and 8.5A through 8.5F). These averages show that some species tend to have denser crowns than others (Randolph 2006, Zarnoch and others 2004). Ongoing research is aimed at identifying the crown conditions that are normal for various species so that healthy and unhealthy crown conditions can be quantified more accurately.

(A)

Percent crown dieback;
plot averages

○   0 – 9
◉   10 – 20
●   21 – 100

Figure 8.3—Crown dieback plot averages for major softwood species of the Eastern United States: (A) spruce and balsam fir, (B) eastern white pine and red pine, (C) northern white-cedar, (D) loblolly and shortleaf pine, (E) Virginia pine, and (F) longleaf and slash pine. Plot locations are approximate. (Data source: U.S. Department of Agriculture Forest Service, FIA Program) (continued to next page)

(B)

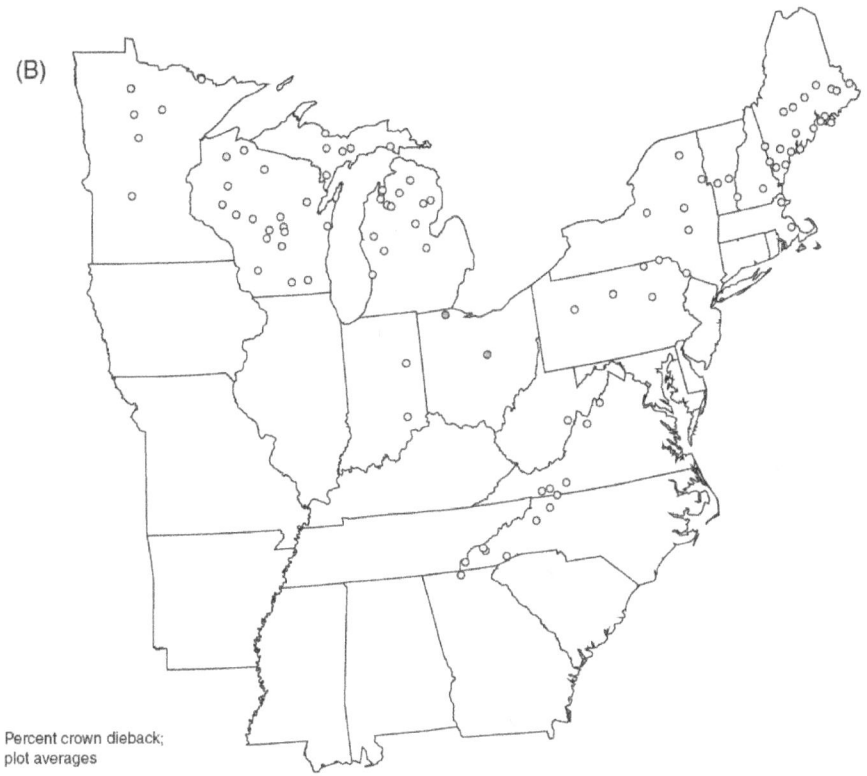

Percent crown dieback;
plot averages

○   0 – 9
◉   10 – 20
●   21 – 100

Figure 8.3 (continued)—Crown dieback plot averages for major softwood species of the Eastern United States: (A) spruce and balsam fir, (B) eastern white pine and red pine, (C) northern white-cedar, (D) loblolly and shortleaf pine, (E) Virginia pine, and (F) longleaf and slash pine. Plot locations are approximate. (Data source: U.S. Department of Agriculture Forest Service, FIA Program) (continued to next page)

(C)

Percent crown dieback;
plot averages

○   0 – 9
◉   10 – 20
●   21 – 100

Figure 8.3 (continued)—Crown dieback plot averages for major softwood species of the Eastern United States: (A) spruce and balsam fir, (B) eastern white pine and red pine, (C) northern white-cedar, (D) loblolly and shortleaf pine, (E) Virginia pine, and (F) longleaf and slash pine. Plot locations are approximate. (Data source: U.S. Department of Agriculture Forest Service, FIA Program) (continued to next page)

(D)

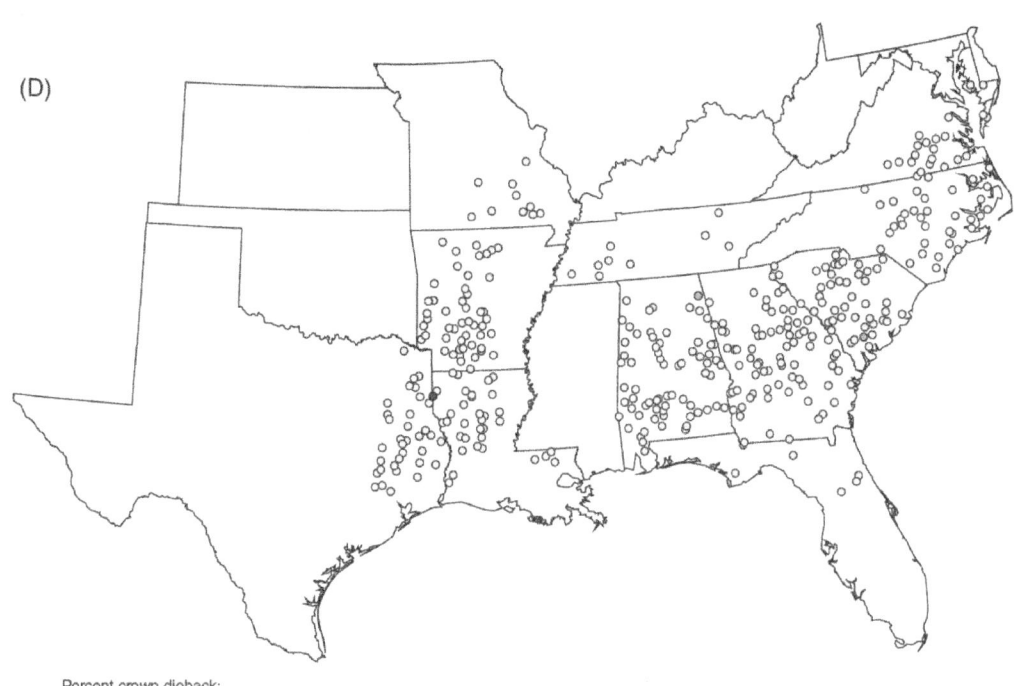

Percent crown dieback;
plot averages

○   0 –   9
◉ 10 – 20
● 21 – 100

Figure 8.3 (continued)—Crown dieback plot averages for major softwood species of the Eastern United States: (A) spruce and balsam fir, (B) eastern white pine and red pine, (C) northern white-cedar, (D) loblolly and shortleaf pine, (E) Virginia pine, and (F) longleaf and slash pine. Plot locations are approximate. (Data source: U.S. Department of Agriculture Forest Service, FIA Program) (continued to next page)

(E)

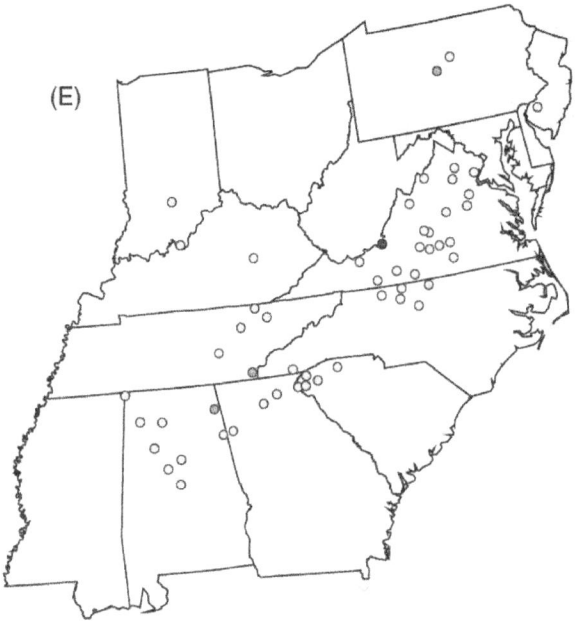

Percent crown dieback;
plot averages

○   0 – 9
◉   10 – 20
●   21 – 100

Figure 8.3 (continued)—Crown dieback plot averages for major softwood species of the Eastern United States: (A) spruce and balsam fir, (B) eastern white pine and red pine, (C) northern white-cedar, (D) loblolly and shortleaf pine, (E) Virginia pine, and (F) longleaf and slash pine. Plot locations are approximate. (Data source: U.S. Department of Agriculture Forest Service, FIA Program) (continued to next page)

(F)

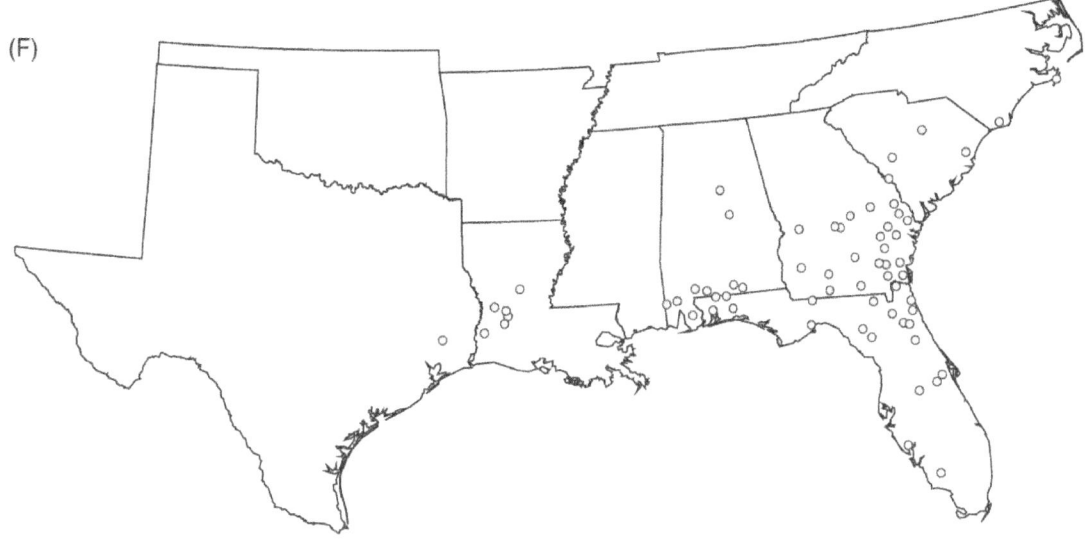

Percent crown dieback;
plot averages

○   0 – 9
◉   10 – 20
●   21 – 100

*Figure 8.3 (continued)—Crown dieback plot averages for major
softwood species of the Eastern United States: (A) spruce and balsam
fir, (B) eastern white pine and red pine, (C) northern white-cedar,
(D) loblolly and shortleaf pine, (E) Virginia pine, and (F) longleaf
and slash pine. Plot locations are approximate. (Data source: U.S.
Department of Agriculture Forest Service, FIA Program)*

(A)

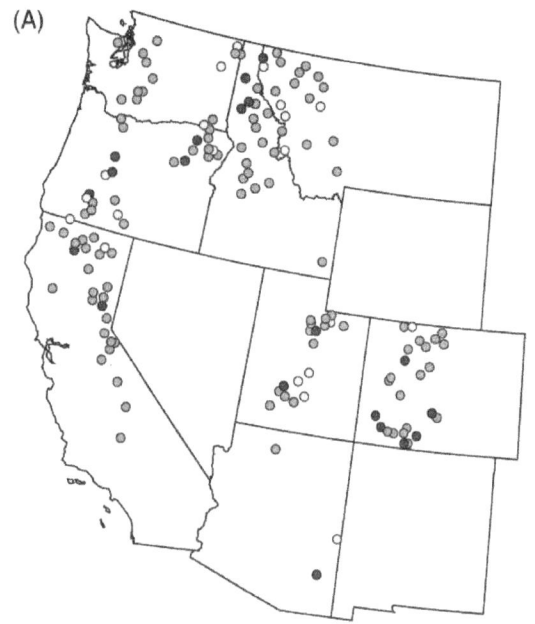

(B)

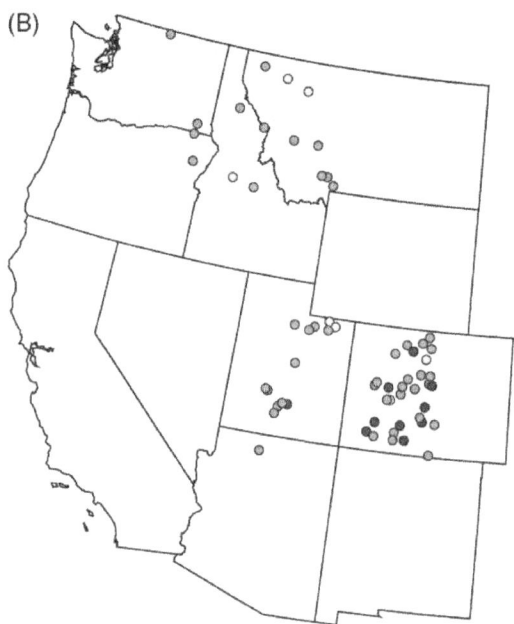

Percent crown density;
plot averages

○   0 – 35
◉   36 – 55
●   56 – 100

Percent crown density;
plot averages

○   0 – 35
◉   36 – 55
●   56 – 100

*Figure 8.4—Crown density plot averages for major softwood species
of the Western United States: (A) true fir, (B) Englemann spruce
and other spruces, (C) lodgepole pine, (D) pinyon pine and juniper,
(E) Douglas-fir, and (F) ponderosa and Jeffrey pine. Plot locations
are approximate. (Data source: U.S. Department of Agriculture
Forest Service, FIA Program) (continued to next page)*

(C)

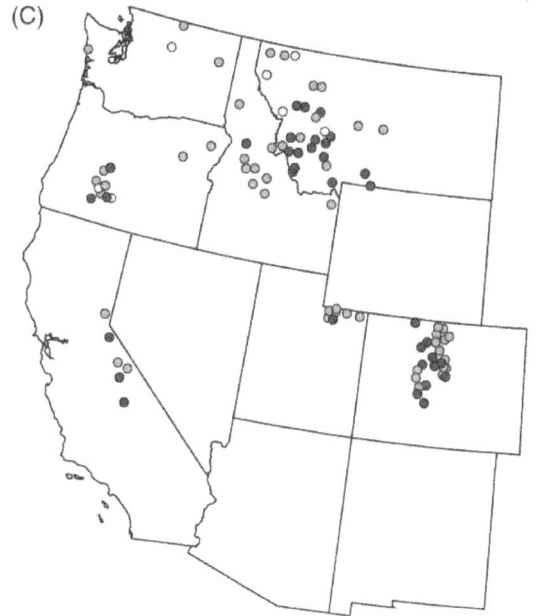

Percent crown density;
plot averages

○   0 – 35
◐   36 – 55
●   56 – 100

(D)

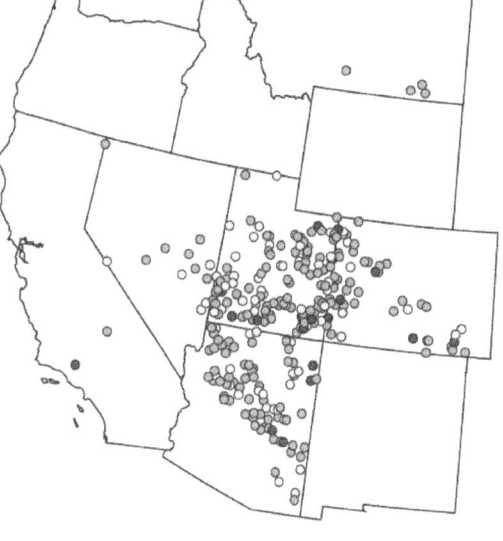

Percent crown density;
plot averages

○   0 – 35
◐   36 – 55
●   56 – 100

*Figure 8.4 (continued)—Crown density plot averages for major
softwood species of the Western United States: (A) true fir,
(B) Englemann spruce and other spruces, (C) lodgepole pine, (D) pinyon
pine and juniper, (E) Douglas-fir, and (F) ponderosa and Jeffrey pine.
Plot locations are approximate. (Data source: U.S. Department of
Agriculture Forest Service, FIA Program) (continued to next page)*

(E)

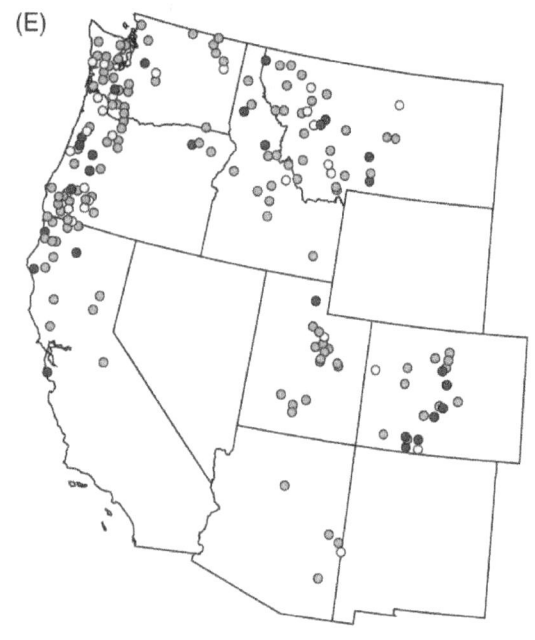

(F)

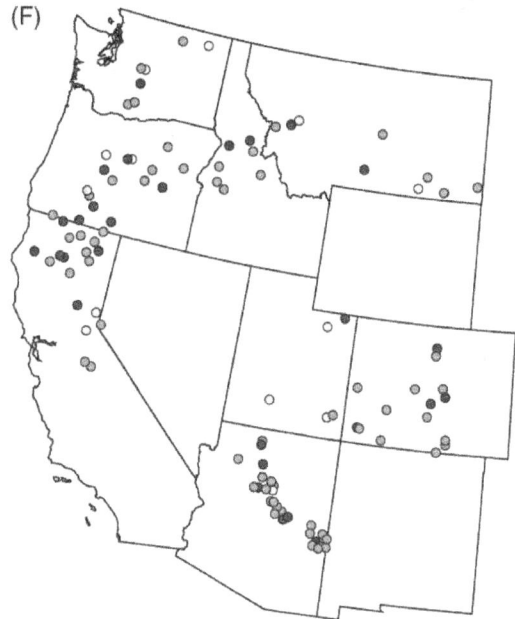

Percent crown density;
plot averages

○   0 – 35
◐   36 – 55
●   56 – 100

Percent crown density;
plot averages

○   0 – 35
◐   36 – 55
●   56 – 100

Figure 8.4 (continued)—Crown density plot averages for major softwood species of the Western United States: (A) true fir, (B) Englemann spruce and other spruces, (C) lodgepole pine, (D) pinyon pine and juniper, (E) Douglas-fir, and (F) ponderosa and Jeffrey pine. Plot locations are approximate. (Data source: U.S. Department of Agriculture Forest Service, FIA Program)

(A)

Percent crown density;
plot averages

○   0 – 35
◉   36 – 55
●   56 – 100

*Figure 8.5—Crown density plot averages for major softwood species
of the Eastern United States: (A) spruce and balsam fir, (B) eastern
white pine and red pine, (C) northern white-cedar, (D) loblolly and
shortleaf pine, (E) Virginia pine, and (F) longleaf and slash pine.
Plot locations are approximate. (Data source: U.S. Department of
Agriculture Forest Service, FIA Program) (continued to next page)*

(B)

Percent crown density;
plot averages

○   0 – 35
◐   36 – 55
●   56 – 100

Figure 8.5 (continued)—Crown density plot averages for major softwood
species of the Eastern United States: (A) spruce and balsam fir, (B) eastern
white pine and red pine, (C) northern white-cedar, (D) loblolly and
shortleaf pine, (E) Virginia pine, and (F) longleaf and slash pine. Plot
locations are approximate. (Data source: U.S. Department of Agriculture
Forest Service, FIA Program) (continued to next page)

(C)

Percent crown density;
plot averages

○   0 – 35
◉   36 – 55
●   56 – 100

Figure 8.5 (continued)—Crown density plot averages for major softwood species of the Eastern United States: (A) spruce and balsam fir, (B) eastern white pine and red pine, (C) northern white-cedar, (D) loblolly and shortleaf pine, (E) Virginia pine, and (F) longleaf and slash pine. Plot locations are approximate. (Data source: U.S. Department of Agriculture Forest Service, FIA Program) (continued to next page)

(D)

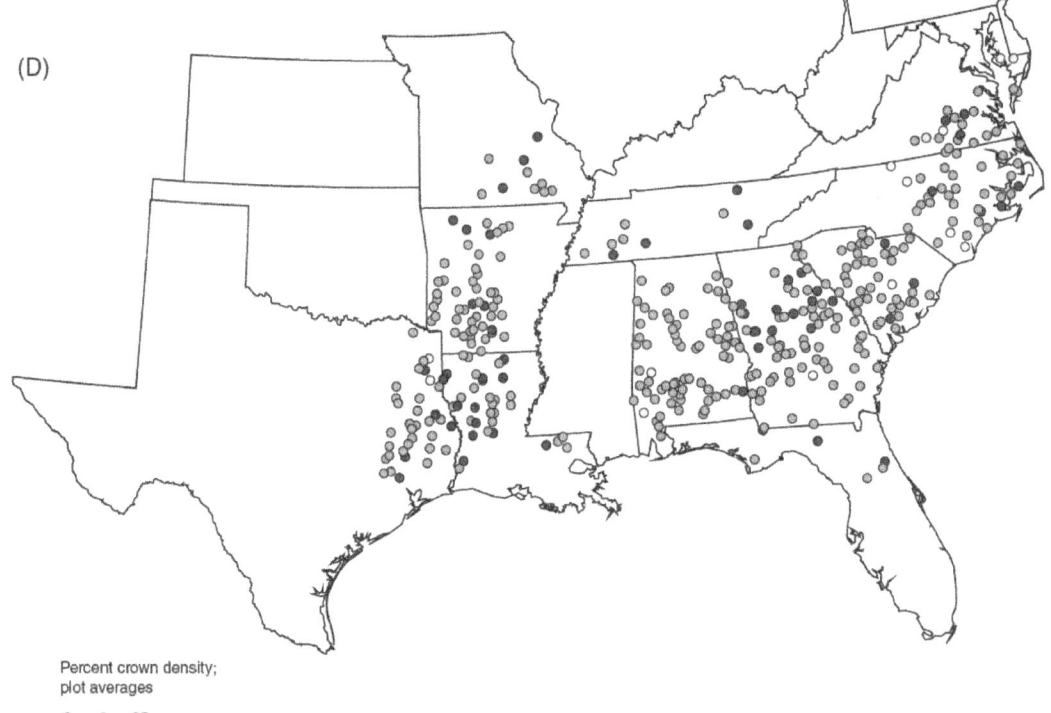

Percent crown density;
plot averages

○   0 – 35
◓   36 – 55
●   56 – 100

Figure 8.5 (continued)—Crown density plot averages for major softwood species of the Eastern United States: (A) spruce and balsam fir, (B) eastern white pine and red pine, (C) northern white-cedar, (D) loblolly and shortleaf pine, (E) Virginia pine, and (F) longleaf and slash pine. Plot locations are approximate. (Data source: U.S. Department of Agriculture Forest Service, FIA Program) (continued to next page)

(E)

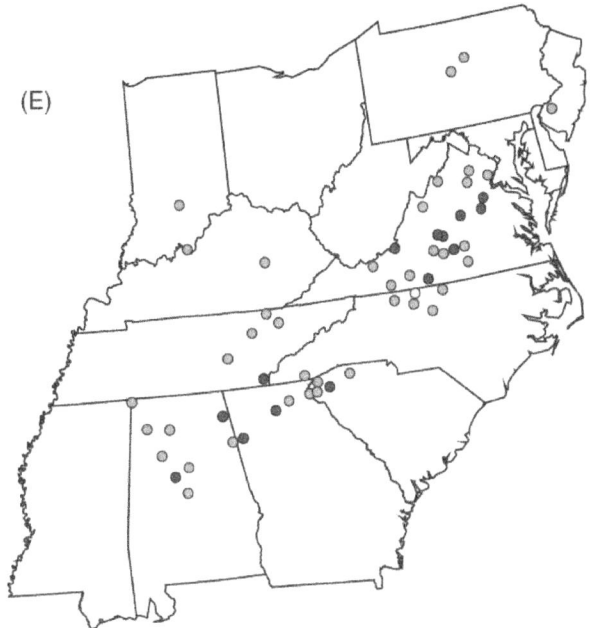

Percent crown density;
plot averages

○   0 – 35
◐ 36 – 55
● 56 – 100

*Figure 8.5 (continued)—Crown density plot
averages for major softwood species of the Eastern
United States: (A) spruce and balsam fir,
(B) eastern white pine and red pine, (C) northern
white-cedar, (D) loblolly and shortleaf pine,
(E) Virginia pine, and (F) longleaf and slash pine.
Plot locations are approximate. (Data source: U.S.
Department of Agriculture Forest Service,
FIA Program) (continued to next page)*

(F)

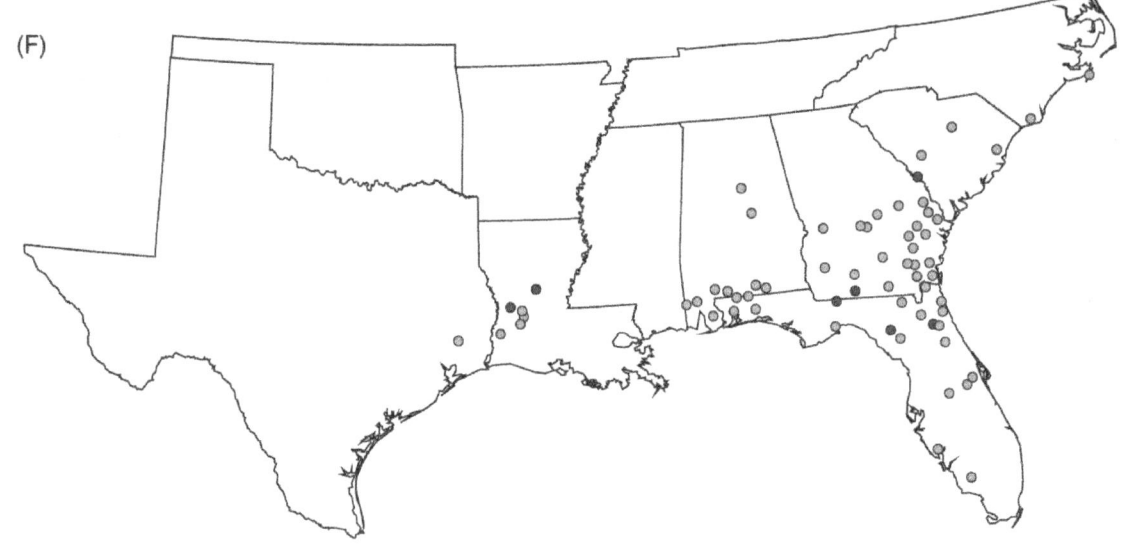

Percent crown density;
plot averages

○   0 – 35
◍   36 – 55
●   56 – 100

*Figure 8.5 (continued)—Crown density plot averages for major
softwood species of the Eastern United States: (A) spruce and balsam
fir, (B) eastern white pine and red pine, (C) northern white-cedar,
(D) loblolly and shortleaf pine, (E) Virginia pine, and (F) longleaf
and slash pine. Plot locations are approximate. (Data source: U.S.
Department of Agriculture Forest Service, FIA Program)*

Hardwoods—Figures 8.6A and 8.6B show plot-level crown dieback and foliage transparency averages across the conterminous United States for the hardwood species group. Plot-level averages for crown dieback were typically <10 percent with only a few scattered plots averaging more than 20 percent dieback. Foliage transparency averages were mostly below 40 percent. Crown dieback averages were relatively high in Arizona and Texas, and foliage transparency averages were relatively high in Texas and northern Minnesota. The high levels of dieback in Arizona and the high levels of dieback and transparency in Texas occurred primarily in a mixture of western woodland species including Arizona white oak, Gambel oak, and silverleaf oak in Arizona and honey mesquite in Texas.

Species-specific plot averages in the East (fig. 8.7) indicated that the trees in the northern Minnesota plots with relatively high foliage transparency averages were primarily cottonwood and aspen species. Plot averages for the cottonwood and aspen trees ranged between 12.9 and 99.0 percent (fig. 8.7D). In Minnesota, 12.7 percent of the cottonwood-aspen plots had averages >40 percent, but only 5.2 percent of the cottonwood-aspen plots

outside of Minnesota had foliage transparency averages >40 percent. During the data collection period, the forest tent caterpillar caused heavy defoliation in northern Minnesota forests. This was accompanied by drought and spring frosts at the time of aspen leaf break. These events contributed to aspen mortality and dieback on 50,000 acres across northern Minnesota in 2004 (Minnesota Department of Natural Resources, Division of Forestry; U.S. Department of Agriculture Forest Service 2006), and may help explain the high foliage transparency averages. In addition to these weather and insect events, tree senescence may also be contributing to the high foliage transparency averages. The 2005 annual report of forest health conditions in Minnesota noted that many of the thinly foliated aspen trees were the largest and oldest trees on the sites (Minnesota Department of Natural Resources, Division of Forestry; U.S. Department of Agriculture Forest Service 2006). The ages at which aspens begin to decline are 55 to 60 years for quaking aspen and 50 to 70 years for bigtooth aspen (Laidly 1990, Perala 1990). The highest foliage transparency averages were observed on plots in stands aged 55 to 70 years, though not all plots in this age range had elevated levels of foliage transparency (fig. 8.8).

(A)

Percent crown dieback;
plot averages

○ 0 – 9
◉ 10 – 20
● 21 – 100

Figure 8.6—Crown dieback (A) and foliage transparency plot (B) averages for hardwood trees in the United States. Plot locations are approximate. (Data source: U.S. Department of Agriculture Forest Service, FIA Program) (continued to next page)

(B)

Percent foliage crown
transparency; plot averages

○   0 – 20
◉   21 – 40
●   41 – 100

*Figure 8.6 (continued)—Crown dieback (A) and foliage
transparency plot (B) averages for hardwood trees in the
United States. Plot locations are approximate. (Data source:
U.S. Department of Agriculture Forest Service, FIA Program)*

(A)

Percent foliage transparency;
plot averages

○   0 – 20
◉   21 – 40
●   41 – 100

Figure 8.7—Foliage transparency plot averages for major hardwood species
of the Eastern United States: (A) maples, (B) hickories, (C) American beech,
(D) cottonwood and aspen, (E) red oaks, and (F) white oaks. Plot locations
are approximate. (Data source: U.S. Department of Agriculture Forest
Service, FIA Program) (continued to next page)

(B)

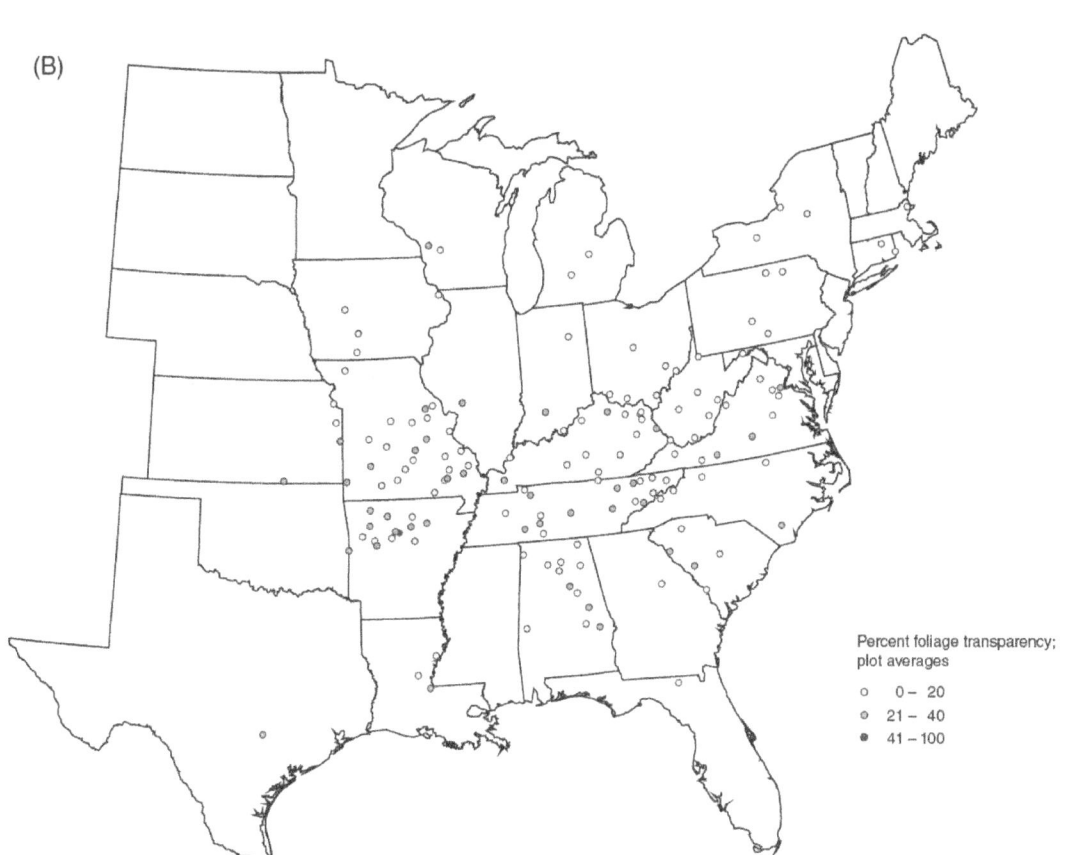

Percent foliage transparency;
plot averages

○　　0 – 20
◓　 21 – 40
●　 41 – 100

Figure 8.7 (continued)—Foliage transparency plot averages for major hardwood species of the Eastern United States: (A) maples, (B) hickories, (C) American beech, (D) cottonwood and aspen, (E) red oaks, and (F) white oaks. Plot locations are approximate. (Data source: U.S. Department of Agriculture Forest Service, FIA Program) (continued to next page)

(C)

Percent foliage transparency;
plot averages

○   0 – 20

◉   21 – 40

●   41 – 100

Figure 8.7 (continued)—Foliage transparency plot averages for major hardwood species of the Eastern United States: (A) maples, (B) hickories, (C) American beech, (D) cottonwood and aspen, (E) red oaks, and (F) white oaks. Plot locations are approximate. (Data source: U.S. Department of Agriculture Forest Service, FIA Program) (continued to next page)

(D)

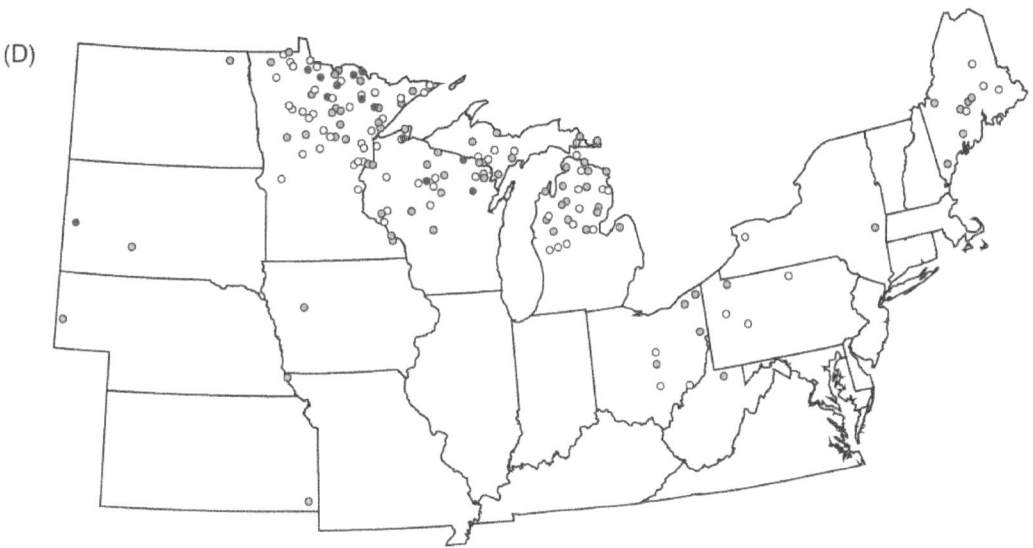

Percent foliage transparency;
plot averages

○   0 – 20
◉   21 – 40
●   41 – 100

*Figure 8.7 (continued)—Foliage transparency plot averages
for major hardwood species of the Eastern United States:
(A) maples, (B) hickories, (C) American beech, (D) cottonwood
and aspen, (E) red oaks, and (F) white oaks. Plot locations are
approximate. (Data source: U.S. Department of Agriculture
Forest Service, FIA Program) (continued to next page)*

(E)

Percent foliage transparency;
plot averages

○   0 – 20
◉   21 – 40
●   41 – 100

*Figure 8.7 (continued)—Foliage transparency plot averages for major
hardwood species of the Eastern United States: (A) maples, (B) hickories,
(C) American beech, (D) cottonwood and aspen, (E) red oaks, and (F) white
oaks. Plot locations are approximate. (Data source: U.S. Department of
Agriculture Forest Service, FIA Program) (continued to next page)*

(F)

Percent foliage transparency;
plot averages

○   0 – 20
◉   21 – 40
●   41 – 100

*Figure 8.7 (continued)—Foliage transparency plot averages for
major hardwood species of the Eastern United States: (A) maples,
(B) hickories, (C) American beech, (D) cottonwood and aspen, (E) red
oaks, and (F) white oaks. Plot locations are approximate. (Data source:
U.S. Department of Agriculture Forest Service, FIA Program)*

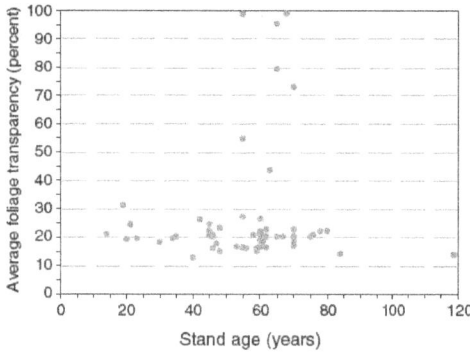

Figure 8.8—Foliage transparency plot averages by stand age for the cottonwood-aspen species group in Minnesota. (Data source: U.S. Department of Agriculture Forest Service, FIA Program)

Other Eastern species groups exhibited spatial clusterings of elevated average dieback (fig. 8.9) and transparency (fig. 8.7). Relatively high levels of red oak (see appendix table A.1), foliage transparency, and crown dieback were clustered in Missouri (figs. 8.7E and 8.9E). There was also a clustering of high dieback levels for maple in eastern Maine (fig. 8.9A), for American beech in New England (fig. 8.9C) and for white oaks (see appendix table A.1) in Pennsylvania and Virginia (fig. 8.9F). There were no outstanding spatial patterns of relatively poor crown condition in hardwoods in the Western United States (figs. 8.10 and 8.11).

The relatively poor condition of red oak crowns in Missouri is likely related to the documented ongoing decline of red oak stands across much of the State (U.S. Department of Agriculture Forest Service 2006). Drought conditions, increasing tree ages, high stand densities, and the red oak borer have contributed to the decline (U.S. Department of Agriculture Forest Service 2003, 2004) and may partially explain the poor crown conditions seen in red oaks.

Relatively high levels of dieback in white oaks in Pennsylvania and Virginia may be the result of gypsy moth defoliation and weather events. A major gypsy moth outbreak occurred in central and southern Pennsylvania during 2000. Defoliation was heavy in both Pennsylvania and Virginia in 2000 and 2001 (U.S. Department

(A)

Percent crown dieback;
plot averages

○   0 –   9
◔ 10 – 20
● 21 – 100

Figure 8.9—Crown dieback plot averages for major hardwood species
of the Eastern United States: (A) maples, (B) hickories, (C) American
beech, (D) cottonwood and aspen, (E) red oaks, and (F) white oaks.
Plot locations are approximate. (Data source: U.S. Department of
Agriculture Forest Service, FIA Program) (continued to next page)

(B)

Percent crown dieback;
plot averages

○   0 – 9
◉   10 – 20
●   21 – 100

*Figure 8.9 (continued)—Crown dieback plot averages for major
hardwood species of the Eastern United States: (A) maples, (B) hickories,
(C) American beech, (D) cottonwood and aspen, (E) red oaks, and (F) white
oaks. Plot locations are approximate. (Data source: U.S. Department of
Agriculture Forest Service, FIA Program) (continued to next page)*

(C)

Percent crown dieback;
plot averages

○   0 – 9
◉   10 – 20
●   21 – 100

*Figure 8.9 (continued)—Crown dieback plot averages for major
hardwood species of the Eastern United States: (A) maples, (B) hickories,
(C) American beech, (D) cottonwood and aspen, (E) red oaks, and (F)
white oaks. Plot locations are approximate. (Data source: U.S. Department
of Agriculture Forest Service, FIA Program) (continued to next page)*

(D)

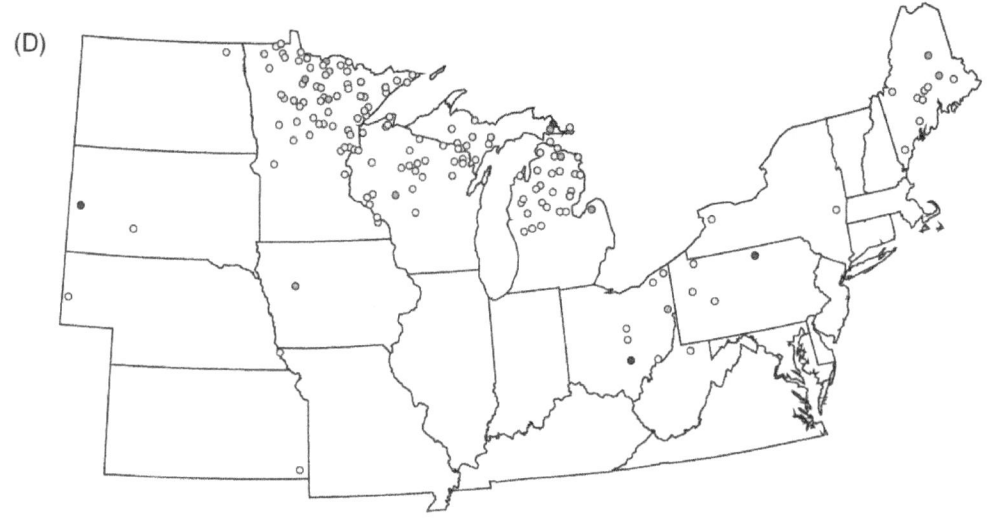

Percent crown dieback;
plot averages

○   0 – 9
◉   10 – 20
●   21 – 100

Figure 8.9 (continued)—Crown dieback plot averages for major hardwood species of the Eastern United States: (A) maples, (B) hickories, (C) American beech, (D) cottonwood and aspen, (E) red oaks, and (F) white oaks. Plot locations are approximate. (Data source: U.S. Department of Agriculture Forest Service, FIA Program) (continued to next page)

(E)

Percent crown dieback;
plot averages

○   0 – 9
◐   10 – 20
●   21 – 100

*Figure 8.9 (continued)—Crown dieback plot averages for major
hardwood species of the Eastern United States: (A) maples, (B) hickories,
(C) American beech, (D) cottonwood and aspen, (E) red oaks, and (F)
white oaks. Plot locations are approximate. (Data source: U.S. Department
of Agriculture Forest Service, FIA Program) (continued to next page)*

(F)

Percent crown dieback;
plot averages

○   0 – 9
◉   10 – 20
●   21 – 100

*Figure 8.9 (continued)—Crown dieback plot averages for major
hardwood species of the Eastern United States: (A) maples,
(B) hickories, (C) American beech, (D) cottonwood and aspen, (E) red
oaks, and (F) white oaks. Plot locations are approximate. (Data source:
U.S. Department of Agriculture Forest Service, FIA Program)*

(A)

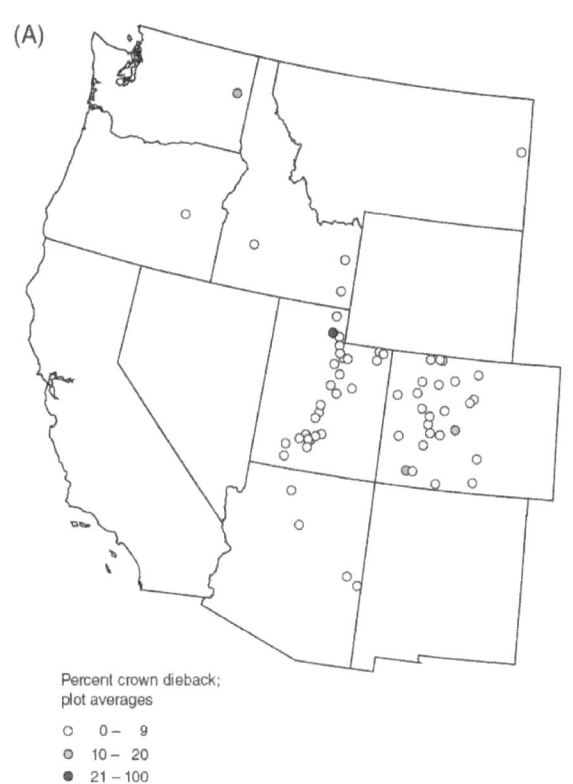

Percent crown dieback;
plot averages

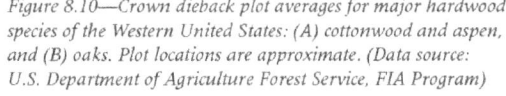

(B)

Percent crown dieback;
plot averages

○ 0 – 9
◐ 10 – 20
● 21 – 100

*Figure 8.10—Crown dieback plot averages for major hardwood
species of the Western United States: (A) cottonwood and aspen,
and (B) oaks. Plot locations are approximate. (Data source:
U.S. Department of Agriculture Forest Service, FIA Program)*

(A)

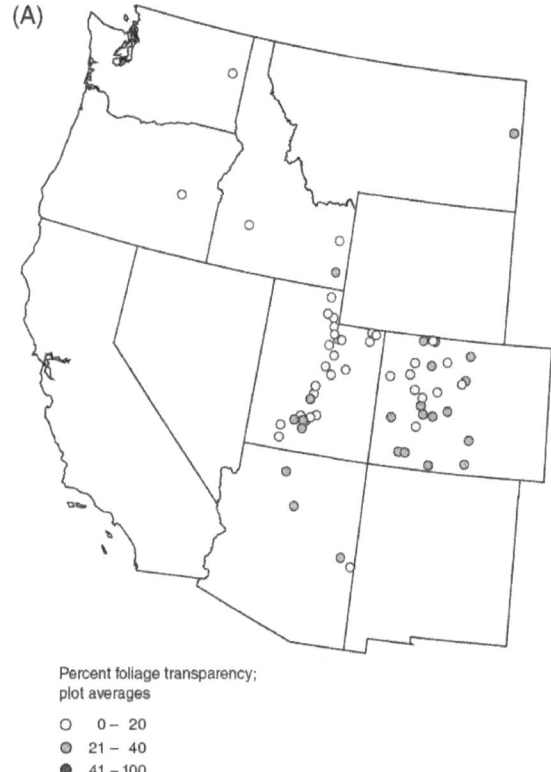

Percent foliage transparency;
plot averages

○   0 – 20
◑   21 – 40
●   41 – 100

(B)

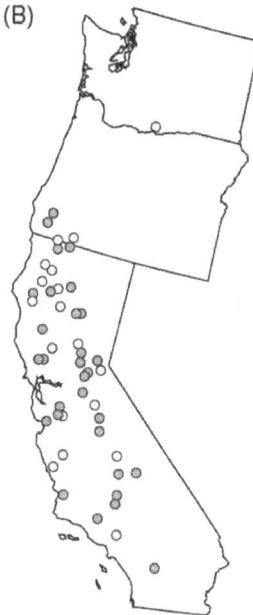

Percent foliage transparency;
plot averages

○   0 – 20
◑   21 – 40
●   41 – 100

*Figure 8.11—Foliage transparency plot averages for major
hardwood species of the Western United States: (A) cottonwood and
aspen, and (B) oaks. Plot locations are approximate. (Data source:
U.S. Department of Agriculture Forest Service, FIA Program)*

of Agriculture Forest Service 2002) (U.S. Department of Agriculture Forest Service; Pennsylvania Department of Conservation and Natural Resources, Bureau of Forestry 2001), and in Pennsylvania, the effects of the gypsy moth may have been exacerbated by droughty conditions between 1998 and 2002 (U.S. Department of Agriculture Forest Service; Pennsylvania Department of Conservation and Natural Resources, Bureau of Forestry 2001, 2003).

High plot-level average dieback for American beech in New England is likely the result of beech bark disease. Beech bark disease is an insect-fungus complex consisting of the beech scale insect and two species of *Neonectria* fungi (*N. faginata* and *N. ditissima*). Trees infected with these organisms often exhibit dieback and thin crowns before succumbing to mortality (Houston and O'Brien 1983). Beech bark disease complex has spread throughout New England (Morin and others 2003) and has been described as a chronic problem in Maine (U.S. Department of Agriculture Forest Service; Maine Forest Service 2004). Lingering effects of the 1998 ice storm that crossed Maine, New Hampshire,

Vermont, and New York may also be evident in the high dieback averages. Though the ice storm caused considerable crown damage among all species, American beech was the most uniformly impacted (Miller-Weeks and others 1999). Most species quickly rebuilt their crowns in the years following the storm, but American beech had shown little recovery by 2002 (U.S. Department of Agriculture Forest Service; Maine Forest Service 2003).

Possible explanations for the elevated levels of maple dieback in eastern Maine are less obvious. The maple plots with the highest dieback levels were dominated by red maple. Throughout most of Maine, large amounts of red maple basal area were in trees with unhealthy crowns between 1993 and 2002 (Steinman 2004). Red maple had poorer crowns than most other species included in Steinman's (2004) analysis. Factors that may be contributing to the high levels of dieback include the 1998 ice storm, from which red maples have been slow to recover (U.S. Department of Agriculture Forest Service; Maine Forest Service 2003), natural or silviculturally induced stand dynamics, and the 1999–2002 drought.

Conclusions

Spatial clusters of high dieback, high transparency, and low crown density were identified for individual species groups in both the Western and Eastern United States. Most of these clusters were located within regions experiencing stress from known agents such as weather events, insect outbreaks, and disease occurrences. Further investigation will be required to identify the stress agents acting upon the few species with relatively poor crown conditions for which no cause is apparent. In addition to answering specific questions such as this, ongoing research is seeking to develop the full utility of the FIA crown condition indicator. Questions about the application of the crown condition indicator to problems such as early detection of declining forest health, growth and mortality prediction models, biomass estimation, and wildlife habitat modeling are being considered. Efforts are being made to determine how "normal" crown condition varies among species and to improve data collection, analysis, and reporting processes in order to increase the usefulness of the crown condition indicator.

Literature Cited

Alerich, C.L.; Klevgard, L.; Liff, C. [and others]. 2005. The forest inventory and analysis database: database description and users guide. Version 2.0. Draft. http://www.ncrs2.fs.fed.us/4801/fiadb/fiadb_documentation/FIADB_DOCUMENTATION.htm. [Date accessed: May 2006].

Houston, D.R.; O'Brien, J.T. 1983. Beech bark disease. For. Insect and Dis. Leafl. 75. Washington, DC: U.S. Department of Agriculture Forest Service. 7 p.

Johnston, W.F. 1990. Northern white-cedar. In: Burns, R.M.; Honkala, B.H., tech. coords. Silvics of North America: 1. Conifers; 2. Hardwoods. Agric. Handb. 654. Washington, DC: U.S. Department of Agriculture Forest Service: 580–589.

Laidly, P.R. 1990. Bigtooth aspen. In: Burns, R.M.; Honkala, B.H., tech. coords. Silvics of North America: 1. Conifers; 2. Hardwoods. Agric. Handb. 654. Washington, DC: U.S. Department of Agriculture Forest Service: 544–550.

Lombard, P.J. 2004. Drought conditions in Maine, 1999–2002: a historical perspective. Water-Resour. Invest. Rep. 03–4310. Augusta, ME: U.S. Department of the Interior, Geological Survey. 36 p.

McRoberts, R.E.; Holden, G.R.; Nelson, M.D. [and others]. 2005. Estimating and circumventing the effects of perturbing and swapping inventory plot locations. Journal of Forestry. 103(6): 275–279.

Miller-Weeks, M.; Eager, C.; Peterson, C.M. [and others]. 1999. The northeastern ice storm 1998: a forest damage assessment for New York, Vermont, New Hampshire, and Maine. [Place of publication unknown]: North East State Foresters Association. 32 p. In cooperation with: U.S. Department of Agriculture Forest Service, State and Private Forestry. http://www.fs.fed.us/na/durham/ice/public/pub_file/ice99.pdf. [Date accessed: June 21, 2006].

Millers, I.; Anderson, R.; Burkman, W.; Hoffard, W. 1992. Crown condition rating guide. [Place of publication unknown]: U.S. Department of Agriculture Forest Service, State and Private Forestry, Northeastern Area and Southern Region. 37 p.

Minnesota Department of Natural Resources, Division of Forestry; U.S. Department of Agriculture Forest Service. 2006. Forest health highlights in Minnesota for 2005. 14 p. http://fhm.fs.fed.us/fhh/fhh-05/mn/mn_05.pdf. [Date accessed: May 2006].

Morin, R.S.; Liebhold, A.M.; Lister, A. [and others]. 2003. Mapping susceptibility and spread associated with beech bark disease [poster]. In: 2003 Forest health monitoring working group meeting. http://fhm.fs.fed.us/posters/posters03/bbdriskposter.pdf. [Date accessed: May 2006].

Perala, D.A. 1990. Quaking aspen. In: Burns, R.M.; Honkala, B.H., tech. coords. Silvics of North America: 1. Conifers; 2. Hardwoods. Agric. Handb. 654. Washington, DC: U.S. Department of Agriculture Forest Service: 555–569.

Randolph, K.C. 2006. Descriptive statistics of tree crown condition in the Southern United States and impacts on data analysis and interpretation. Gen. Tech. Rep. SRS–94. Asheville, NC: U.S. Department of Agriculture Forest Service, Southern Research Station. 17 p.

Shaw, J.D.; Steed, B.E.; DeBlander, L.T. 2005. Forest inventory and analysis (FIA) annual inventory answers the question: what is happening to pinyon-juniper woodlands? Journal of Forestry. 103(6): 280–285.

Steinman, J. 2000. Tracking the health of trees over time on forest health monitoring plots. In: Hansen, M.; Burk, T., eds. Integrated tools for natural resources inventories in the 21st century: Proceedings of the IUFRO conference. Gen. Tech. Rep. NC–212. St. Paul, MN: U.S. Department of Agriculture Forest Service, North Central Research Station: 334–339.

Steinman, J. 2004. Forest health monitoring in the Northeastern United States: disturbances and conditions during 1993–2002. NA–TP–01–04. Newtown Square, PA: U.S. Department of Agriculture Forest Service, Northeastern Area, State and Private Forestry. 46 p.

U.S. Department of Agriculture Forest Service. 2002. Forest health highlights - 2001 Virginia. http://www.fs.fed.us/r8/foresthealth/cooperators/states/fh_highlights/2001/va/va.html. [Date accessed: May 2006].

U.S. Department of Agriculture Forest Service. 2003. Missouri forest health highlights 2002. http://fhm.fs.fed. us/fhh/fhh-02/mo/mo_02.htm. [Date accessed: May 2006].

U.S. Department of Agriculture Forest Service. 2004. Missouri forest health highlights 2003. http://fhm.fs.fed. us/fhh/fhh-03/mo/mo_03.htm. [Date accessed: May 2006].

U.S. Department of Agriculture Forest Service. 2005. Forest insect and disease conditions in the United States 2004. Washington, DC: U.S. Department of Agriculture Forest Service, Forest Health Protection. 142 p.

U.S. Department of Agriculture Forest Service. 2006. Missouri forest health 2005 highlights. 9 p. http://fhm. fs.fed.us/fhh/fhh-05/mo/mo_05.pdf. [Date accessed: May 2006].

U.S. Department of Agriculture Forest Service; Maine Forest Service. 2003. 2002 Forest health highlights Maine. 2 p. http://fhm.fs.fed.us/fhh/fhh-02/me/me_02.pdf. [Date accessed: May 2006].

U.S. Department of Agriculture Forest Service; Maine Forest Service. 2004. 2003 Forest health highlights Maine. 2 p. http://fhm.fs.fed.us/fhh/fhh-03/me/me_03.pdf. [Date accessed: May 2006].

U.S. Department of Agriculture Forest Service; Pennsylvania Department of Conservation and Natural Resources, Bureau of Forestry. 2001. Pennsylvania forest health highlights (2000). 2 p. http://fhm.fs.fed.us/fhh/fhh-00/pa/ pa2000.pdf. [Date accessed: May 2006].

U.S. Department of Agriculture Forest Service; Pennsylvania Department of Conservation and Natural Resources, Bureau of Forestry. 2003. Pennsylvania - 2002 forest health highlights. 2 p. http://fhm.fs.fed.us/fhh/fhh-02/pa/ pa2002.pdf. [Date accessed: May 2006].

Zarnoch, S.J.; Bechtold, W.A.; Stolte, K.W. 2004. Using crown condition variables as indicators of forest health. Canadian Journal of Forest Research. 34: 1057–1070.

Forest Health Monitoring (FHM), together with cooperating researchers both in and outside of the Forest Service, continues to investigate a variety of issues relating to forest health. This report provides some of the latest analyses and results. The broad range of indicators presented demonstrates one reason it can be difficult to draw general conclusions about the condition of U.S. forests.

A number of stressors are affecting U.S. forests to varying degrees. Drought periodically affects nearly all U.S. forests to some extent. In 2005, the worst drought (9 months) occurred in ecoregion section M332G—Blue Mountains. Over the past decade (1996–2005), much of the Interior West of the United States was considerably more droughty than the historic average. Much of the Southeast was slightly more droughty than the historic average over the same period. With some exceptions, ecoregion sections of the remainder of the Eastern United States as well as the West Coast experienced the expected amount of drought, or less, over that period.

Fire also periodically affects many U.S. forests, and managing the risk of catastrophic fire is an important issue. An analysis of lightning as an ignition source for forest fires suggests that lightning flash density can serve as a predictor of where forest fires are likely to occur in the Eastern United States and in parts of the West. Therefore, in those areas lightning data might be used as a tool for prioritizing efforts to reduce fuel loads and, thus, reduce the risk of wildfire.

Anthropogenic stressors, such as air pollution, are a concern because of possible impacts on forest health and productivity. Analyses of National Atmospheric Deposition Program (NADP) pollution data showed a strong eastwest gradient in wet sulfate and nitrogen (NO_3^- and NH_4^+) deposition, with the highest deposition levels being in the Northeast FHM region. Ozone followed a different pattern. SUM06 ozone exposures were highest in the Interior West FHM region. The Forest Inventory and Analysis (FIA) lichens indicator was also used to understand the effects of pollution on forests in the Pacific Northwest (PNW).

Chapter 9. Summary

MARK J. AMBROSE

Although the NADP data show air pollution to be relatively low throughout the PNW, a gradient model relating lichen communities to pollution indicates relatively high levels of nitrogen deposition mostly concentrated in ecoregion section 242A—Willamette Valley and Puget Trough. It is possible that even nitrogen deposition levels that are quite low compared with the Eastern United States are capable of negatively affecting lichen communities. It is also possible that through dry deposition parts of the PNW are receiving much higher nitrogen inputs than are indicated by the wet deposition analysis alone.

A variety of insects and pathogens affect U.S. forests. Many different species of mortality- and defoliation-causing agents were recorded during aerial surveys of the conterminous United States from 1998 through 2004. Analyses of relative exposure to defoliation- and mortality-causing agents identified hotspots of insect and pathogen activity in each FHM region. Of mortality-causing species, southern pine beetle was most frequently observed in the South FHM region and balsam woolly adelgid in the Northeast. In the North Central region, beech bark disease was frequently observed in northern Michigan while mountain pine beetle was observed in the Black Hills of South Dakota. In the Interior West region, mountain pine beetle, Douglas-fir beetle, fir engraver, and spruce beetle were responsible for high relative exposures. In the West Coast FHM region, areas of high mortality were attributed to bark beetles. Continued monitoring of forested areas is important to determine when the activity of insects and pathogens warrants followup investigation or management action.

Both native and exotic insects and pathogens have the potential to damage U.S. forests, but exotic pests, lacking biological controls found in their lands of origin, can be especially harmful. An analysis of quantities of freight coming into the United States and the locations where exotic insects were first discovered showed that several recently introduced exotic insect pests first established themselves in the vicinity of major marine ports. Also, several ecoregions have high proportions of their forested area within 100 miles of marine ports, which might provide venues where newly imported exotic pests can become established in the future.

Crown condition is an indicator of the health of trees because it reflects the amount of tissue available to the tree for photosynthesis. Analyses of FIA crown indicator data showed no areas of outstandingly poor crown condition that would be indicative of large-scale, generalized forest health problems when data from all hardwoods or all softwoods were examined as a group. However, when crown condition was analyzed by tree species group, spatial clusters of plots where trees had high crown dieback, high foliar transparency, or low crown density were identified in both the Western and Eastern United States. Most of these clusters were located within regions experiencing stress from known agents such as weather events, insects, and pathogens. Many of the causal agents co-occurring with clusters of relatively poor crown condition were insects or pathogens specific to certain tree species or genera. Further investigation will be required to identify the causal agents responsible for relatively poor crown conditions in the few species for which no cause is apparent.

The results presented in this report reflect output from FHM's national-scale detection monitoring efforts. It is possible to fail to detect national-scale forest health problems if the indicators being measured do not show a strong signal relative to the natural variability in forest conditions. Whenever a potential forest health problem is discovered through such large-scale analyses, it is important to follow up with more detailed study to verify the findings and determine the extent and seriousness of the issue. Also, it is important to be aware that forest health issues of local or regional importance may exist which, because of their small scale, are not detected in these analyses. Other reports produced by FHM and its partners often address smaller scale forest health issues that are not covered in these national-scale analyses.

Table A.1—Species List

Species group[a]	Species
True fir	*Abies amabilis, A. concolor, A. grandis, A. lasiocarpa, A. lasiocarpa var. arizonica, A. magnifica, A. shastensis, A. procera*
Spruce and balsam fir (East)	*Abies balsamea, Picea glauca, P. mariana, P. rubens*
Engelmann and other spruces (West)	*Picea engelmannii, P. glauca, P. mariana, P. pungens*
Pinyon and juniper	*Juniperus californica, J. coahuilensis, J. deppeana, J. monosperma, J. osteosperma, J. scopulorum, Pinus cembroides, P. discolor, P. edulis, P. monophylla, P. monophylla var. fallax*
Longleaf and slash pines	*Pinus elliottii, P. palustris*
Lodgepole pine	*Pinus contorta*
Loblolly and shortleaf pines	*Pinus echinata, P. taeda*
Ponderosa and jeffrey pines	*Pinus jeffreyi, P. ponderosa*
Eastern white and red pines	*Pinus resinosa, P. strobus*
Virginia pine	*Pinus virginiana*
Douglas-fir	*Pseudotsuga menziesii*
Northern white-cedar	*Thuja occidentalis*
Maple	*Acer barbatum, A. nigrum, A. rubrum, A. saccharinum, A. saccharum*
Hickory	*Carya spp[b], C. alba, C. aquatica, C. cordiformis, C. glabra, C. illinoinensis, C. laciniosa, C. ovata, C. pallida, C. texana*

continued

Table A.1—Species List (continued)

Species group[a]	Species
American beech	*Fagus grandifolia*
Cottonwood and aspen (West)	*Populus angustifolia, P. balsamifera sub. trichocarpa, P. deltoides sub. monilifera, P. tremuloides*
Cottonwood and aspen (East)	*Populus spp.[b], P. balsamifera, P. deltoides, P. deltoides sub. monilifera, P. grandidentata, P. heterophylla, P. tremuloides*
Red oaks	*Quercus buckleyi, Q. coccinea, Q. ellipsoidalis, Q. falcata, Q. hispanica, Q. imbricaria, Q. laurifolia, Q. marilandica, Q. nigra, Q. pagoda, Q. palustris, Q. phellos, Q. rubra, Q. shumardii, Q. velutina*
White oaks	*Quercus alba, Q. bicolor, Q. lyrata, Q. macrocarpa, Q. margarettiae, Q. michauxii, Q. muehlenbergii, Q. prinus, Q. similis, Q. stellata, Q. virginiana*
Western oaks	*Quercus agrifola, Q. chrysolepis, Q. douglasii, Q. garryana, Q. kelloggii, Q. lobata, Q. wislizeni*
Western woodland hardwoods	*Acer glabrum, A. gradidentatum, Cercocarpus ledifolius, Condalia hookeri, Prosopis glandulosa var. torreyana, P. velutina, Quercus arizonica, Q. emoryi, Q. gambelii, Q. grisea, Q. hypoleucoides, Q. oblongifolia, Q. rugosa*

[a]See Alerich and others (2005) for a complete listing of FIA species groups.
[b]Species group includes trees identified to genus only.

Acknowledgments

This research was supported in part through the project "Forest Health Assessment" of Cooperative Agreement SRS 05–CA–11330146–180, project "Forest Health Monitoring, Analysis and Assessment" of research joint venture agreement 06–JV–11330146–124, project "Modeling Uncertainty in Forest Ecosystem Risk Assessments" of research joint venture agreement 06–JV–11330146–123, and project "Forest Health Monitoring and Assessment" of research joint venture agreement 07–JV–11330146–134 between North Carolina State University (this institution is an equal opportunity provider) and the Forest Service, Southern Research Station, Asheville, NC. This research was supported by funds provided by the Forest Service, Southern Research Station, Asheville, NC.

The authors thank the following for their constructive comments: Randall Morin, Borys Tkacz, and Stanley Zarnoch. Individual author acknowledgments: chapter 3—additional review was kindly provided by Jeff Prestemon; chapter 5—Mark Ambrose offered many helpful thoughts and edits on this chapter; additional review was kindly provided by Sally Campbell, Frank Koch, Bruce McCune, Peter Neitlich, and KaDonna Randolph; chapter 8—much appreciation is extended to FIA Spatial Data Services, and especially to Sam Lambert, for assistance in obtaining publicly viewable plot locations.

Author Information

JOHN W. COULSTON, Research Scientist, U.S. Department of Agriculture Forest Service, Southern Research Station, Knoxville, TN 37919

SARAH JOVAN, Postdoctoral Fellow, U.S. Department of Agriculture Forest Service, Pacific Northwest Research Station, Portland, OR 97205

FRANK H. KOCH, Research Assistant Professor, North Carolina State University, Department of Forestry and Environmental Resources, Raleigh, NC 27695

KaDonna C. Randolph, Mathematical Statistician, U.S. Department of Agriculture Forest Service, Southern Research Station, Knoxville, TN 37919